MASTERING THE SHOTGUN

PLATE 1.   The author in the process of running 25 straight at skeet at the newly opened Winchester Franchised Shooting Center at Thunder Mountain, New York.

MASTERING THE SHOTGUN

Richard Alden Knight

Revised Edition, Updated by

Bob Bell

Editor, *Pennsylvania Game News*
Technical Editor, *Gun Digest*

Illustrated with photographs by Pody
and drawings by Harold Bush

A Sunrise Book
E. P. Dutton & Co., Inc. | New York | 1975

201 Park ave, South
New York, N.Y. 10003

Published simultaneously in Canada by Clarke, Irwin & Company
Limited, Toronto and Vancouver
ISBN: 0-87690-177-1
Library of Congress Catalog Card Number: 75-10923

To my late father, John Alden Knight, who taught
me so well in my early years

ACKNOWLEDG-MENTS

As with most books, the work of the author of this one has been largely to correlate the efforts of a great number of people who have given freely of their time, knowledge, and ability. Without their assistance, it is indeed doubtful if this treatise would ever have been written. My heartfelt thanks go to the following people who have helped to make this book a reality:

Bob Lockard was a fount of information whenever I needed him. The boys of Winchester Arms, Jim Rikhoff, Scott Healy, Bill Kelty, and Hank Hunter, proved that a big corporation can and does take the time to make an author's task easier. The roundtable comments freely given at a wonderful goose shoot by Hugh Grey of *Field and Stream* magazine, Charles Dickey of the National Shooting Sports Foundation, and Ted McCawley of Remington Arms confirmed my own beliefs to the point where I had the confidence to set them down on paper. Lastly, my shooting companion and close friend Chuck Matter has spent many hours working with my wife and me to prepare the photographs used in the volume.

My gratitude goes to my wife, Jacqueline, whose professional name, Pody, appears on the title page of this book. Her persistence in recording detail with a camera, her daily belief in my ability to present this work the way it should be presented, and her everlasting devotion to it in its final stages have made it so much easier to believe that what I was doing should be done.

To these people, and to the hundreds of shooting acquaintances I have made over the years (each of whom has taught me just a bit more), my sincere gratitude.

R. A. K.

CONTENTS

FOREWORD

To my way of thinking, the basic purpose behind hunting, once we look beyond the twin realities of sport and enjoyment, lies in the insurmountable fact that man still has the urge to kill buried in his bosom. This urge has been repressed or subordinated by years of civilization and rules of conduct. Yet let a man take firearm in hand and go forth, and the same rules hold that held when his prehistoric ancestor clobbered a passing animal with a stone ax.

We speak of shooting for food, and properly so, for much that is good to eat abounds outdoors. No one can fault you for enjoying a pheasant or a grouse or a woodcock. But one constant remains at all times. To enjoy such delicacies you must kill them. In this simple purpose lies the foundation for this book.

No one who shoots likes to wound or cripple. The clean kill or the slamming of a bird out of the air with a single, all-devastating shot is the dream of the true hunter. This one masterstroke, the ultimate in humane hunting, is the underlying mutual desire of all good gunners. But when we approach this simple fact of killing—and let us address it at its most basic level—we should be masters of our craft. With this in mind, why do we, as hunters, use our tool, the shotgun, with such execrable lack of ability?

The world is overpopulated with poor shotgun shots. If we must establish a yardstick of difficulty, the shotgun actually ranks in the middle of the scale. The .45 automatic pistol, to my way of thinking, is the most difficult; bench shooting the .22 calibers must rank as the easiest. Yet the shotgun, filling a 30-inch circle at 40 yards in its tightest of chokes, and giving you a shot column of 9 to 13 feet in length, is responsible for more missed targets than any other sporting firearm.

I have been blessed with the gift of coordination since I was a boy. I say this because not all of us are. As a result (and with hours of shooting practice to my credit), I have turned into a far better-than-average shotgun shot. This is not a statement stemming from ego, for in the sport of hunting there is no room for ego. Rather it is a simple truth. God save me from the expert, either appointed or self-appointed. I know but one expert, a man who taught me much of what I now know of shooting theory and ballistics, who can actually lay claim to being an accomplished shot. His name is Larry Koller. Larry can shoot anything well. He has forgotten more about theory than many of us will ever learn. With a shotgun, be it on the trap or skeet field or in the brush after fur and feathers, Larry is a master shot. He is the *only* all-around shot I have ever met who can lay claim to the title of expert in every sense of the term.

To become modestly proficient with a shotgun in every department is not difficult. To become a master-hand requires hours of practice—*away* from the skeet and trap field rather than on it. Skill in skeet or trapshooting is no assurance of equal effectiveness in the field. The number of poor game shots who bear good trap and skeet averages is legion.

Many books about shooting have been written, none of which I agree with entirely. Call me a maverick if you will, but I feel that my fellow writers tend to becloud the issues, perhaps to overemphasize them to justify the existence of their book in the field of shooting literature. The simpler you make the basics, the quicker you can teach a pupil to use a shotgun better than passably.

Therefore, this is a book on shotgun shooting—shooting to kill, as well as trapshooting and skeet shooting. In its pages are descriptions of how to shoot or mount a shotgun, all written for the right-handed shooter. If you are left-handed, you will have to reverse the procedures described. Because it is a book on shooting, it is designed with but one purpose in mind. When you shoulder your fowling piece and glance over its barrel or barrels, you will hit that at which you are looking at the time. It is that simple . . . nothing more, nothing less.

MASTERING THE SHOTGUN

1 | IN THE BEGINNING

Shooting to me is more than a sport; it is, in actuality, a way of life. In the peripatetic existence I lead as an outdoor writer, I travel widely. My daily life is spent making my avocation my vocation. My vacations, if such they can be called in a business where nearly every day is a vacation in itself, are spent doing the same things I do when I am working . . . hunting and fishing. I suppose I am the result of training by a father who dedicated me at birth on the altar of outdoor writing. Like it or not, I could not have been a plumber or a doctor or a lawyer. My upbringing was deliberately and carefully planned. While I did not teeth on a shotgun (an expression that has always sounded a bit bizarre to me), I had one when I could stand up under its weight. I killed my first game bird at some ridiculously early age in the dim, unrecollected past. I have been a bug on the subject of hunting ever since.

My father, John Alden Knight, was perhaps the greatest guiding force in my life. An outdoor writer for over thirty years, author of fourteen books on shooting and fishing, and some 500 magazine articles, and originator of the Solunar Tables, the day-by-day forecast of wildlife's cyclic feeding activity, Dad was considered the dean in his field. Elected Outdoorsman of the Year by some 3,600 of his peers in 1963, he was honored by the Winchester Arms Company at a ceremony in New Haven, Connecticut. A patient teacher and a stylist in any field, he gave freely of his time and advice to guide me on the path of outdoor writing.

Dad started me with a shotgun, a cut-down .410 that I was allowed to keep in my room, when I was about six. In my parents' bedroom was a full-length mirror attached to the back of their closet door. This was my checkpoint classroom in gunhandling. The hours I spent standing in front of that mirror, practicing mounting a shotgun to my shoulder, are countless. It was there that I taught myself the sequence of gun throws with which I shall deal later in this book. The mirror gave me visual correction of obvious faults; it made me practice until I found that mounting a gun should be all one motion, a fluid movement fully as involved as a good golf swing, yet by no means as difficult.

Like any youngster, I was obsessed with the need for developing speed in my shooting. My idea of perfection was to mount and fire the gun in a blur of motion, all blended together into one miraculously accurate movement. Wyatt Earp was slow in comparison to my finest efforts before the mirror. That little gun would bust up, go snap, and be down, all in one motion. Imaginary game would pile up around the bedroom to a point it almost makes me blush now to think back upon. I never missed a thing . . . always my target folded gently and settled into that Great Beyond where game birds eventually go when dispatched by a master hunter. My obsession for speed took me nearly ten years to overcome. As a youngster, I couldn't hit my fanny with both hands!

On my sixteenth birthday, truly a momentous occasion in itself, my first personal shotgun was presented to me with great ceremony. It was a Marlin over-and-under, a 16-gauge, all factory-pretty, and cosmolined to the nines. It had a faired trigger guard of which I shall speak in depth later. It was a dream, a beauty . . . and it was mine alone.

Shortly after Christmas that year, Joe Brooks, the nationally known outdoor writer, invited Dad, my uncle (by marriage), and me down to Chesapeake Bay's Back and Middle River district to go blackhead shooting. The Greater Scaup or blackhead is one of the prettiest little ducks that flies; and shooting him with the liberal limit we had then (I believe it was either 10 or 12 birds a day) was a joy. It was my very first duck-shooting trip.

My Marlin had a sharp drop at heel and a recoil that would make a strong man cry. We went into the blind that rainy, blowy, cold morning at the heathenish hour of four. The next hour was spent laying the decoy set, running out the tiller line to toll the ducks up the wind into the main set, and generally getting as wet and as cold as one must to enjoy a day's duck gunning to its fullest. Finally the appointed hour came and the first flock swung in over the decoys, all the birds making the same movements simultaneously, as only scaup can do. In the hours I have spent watching this species fly, I've never known their actions to vary: all heads turn in the same direction, all feet are lowered at the same instant, and all wings are cocked at precisely the same angle.

My uncle had sat on his tailbone all through the decoy-laying period, pleading a poor constitution and a bad back. He had appropriated the

PLATE 2. Learning to shoot accurately was one of the author's youthful trials.

center of the blind and had spent the best part of an hour sipping away on a bottle of Old Popskull to while away the dull, early hours. As the first flock bunched and came into range, we rose in a group. I picked out a bird on my side, led him what I thought was enough, and killed hell out of him. Joe Brooks pulled down a pair, as did Dad. Uncle also shot.

This being my first duck kill, I was delirious with accomplishment. Nothing would do but what I had to hop into the dory and go out to pick up all the ducks. This I did while Uncle helped himself to another portion of snakebite medicine. This also continued throughout the day—everyone doing and Uncle sitting and sipping.

Late in the day—it must have been about 2:00 P.M.—one lone blackhead came over so high he looked like a hummingbird. We had not popped a cap at anything for over an hour, and being young and bored, I swung some fantastic distance ahead of the bird and proceeded to kill him with one or perhaps two pellets through the head. Down he came like an errant comet, slamming into the water directly in front of the blind. By now, I was in seventh heaven. It was then that Uncle cleared his throat, smiled benignly, if not a bit woozily, at the assemblage, and said pompously, "It certainly is nice to see the boy *finally* kill a bird!"

Looking back on this incident now, I can say that I have mellowed with age. At the time, I was set to do battle on the spot. One lesson still remains in full force with me; and never, not once in my whole shooting career, have I ever forgotten the lesson learned that cold day: Drinking and shooting do not mix under any circumstances.

The faired trigger guard on that Marlin, I shall always remember, had such an angle of attack where the receiver joined the underside of the tang that the pulling of the front trigger slammed the fairing back against the first joint of my middle finger. This engineering fault, combined with the horrendous recoil associated with express loads in that misbalanced, poorly bedded piece of shooting equipment, left me that evening with a finger that resembled a banana. Every time it rains, the lumpy bone bruise that still remains by way of scar tissue on that finger aches, serving to remind me that shotguns must fit to be enjoyed.

By the time World War II was beginning in Europe, I had just entered Cornell to study Wildlife Conservation and Management under Dr. Arthur A. Allen, one of the nation's top men in his field. As you can see, my father's groundwork had been well laid. With the advent of hostilities in Hawaii, everything went up in smoke. The war fever gripped us all, and I was not unusual in my class in presenting myself for enlistment in the Corps of Naval Aviation Cadets. In all the fussing about and wondering (as do all youngsters when faced with a "tomorrow we may die" situation which they inevitably over-dramatize) when and where we would be called, I proceeded to bust out of my freshman year in resounding style. Fortunately for my home life and my future relationship with my father (whose hard-earned cash had gone down the drain), I was called up shortly thereafter.

Like the weak-hitting shortstop whose career ended in the minors, I was good field, no hit. I could fly hell out of an airplane, but I was an utter dodo in celestial navigation. Engine theory left me cold, and my inability to apply myself to anything more demanding than taking the controls and flying ended my dreams of wings in short order. Eleven months later, I was sent to boot camp to start all over again. There someone discovered that I could shoot, and in short order I wound up as a trap and skeet instructor at Memphis Naval Air Technical Training Center.

Those were happy days. In my instructor group was a man to whom I am hugely indebted for the patience and work he put into my shooting at trap and skeet. His name is Rudy Etchen, and he was former National Trap Doubles Champion before he joined the Navy. Truly a magnificent trap shot, he used to clean out our pockets each Saturday afternoon on instructors' money shoots. We financed many a happy weekend liberty for Rudy in those days, while we either stayed aboard or went ashore on a shoestring.

Those days of free and unlimited shotgun shells and plenty of time to practice did an amazing thing to my shooting. Gradually I became—if I must say so myself—a good shot. Hell, when you shoot 12 rounds of skeet and trap a day for months, you *have* to learn something! This, combined with dove shooting on the skeet range at daybreak, quail gunning right inside the fence of the mammoth base area, and trips for ducks to the nearby Arkansas rice paddies all led to the making of a shotgun shot.

Shells during the war were in short supply, so short that the bird supply wasn't hit nearly as hard as it had been previously. Shells we had, and this made us instant *personae gratae* at my duck club. It gave us the use of any number of superb quail dogs; it opened the gates at farms whose dove shooting was nearly unbelievable. I have a recollection of sitting on a high spot in an Arkansas rice paddy, shooting *nothing* but right-to-left quartering Mallard drakes to fill out my limit. It was that good. It was also a crucible, a time of fine honing.

Many new gunners speak of lead in the form of so many feet, so many inches. To gauge correctly that indefinable distance you must point your shotgun in front of a moving object to connect it with the charge of shot from your shell had always seemed to me to be the unreachable ultimate in shotgun shooting. When I finally found that there was no such thing as lead, that you put the gun out where it will hit the bird without even think-

PLATE 3.   The author's service experience improved his shooting overnight.

ing about how far you are ahead of it, that was the day that shotgun shooting became a thing of joy.

Development of shooting form, or more correctly a particular method of shooting procedure, is time-consuming work. Trying to sell this method to people who feel that they already know all that there is to know about shotguns, the shooting thereof, and success in the field, is far different. So many theories of shooting have been advanced that seemingly everyone has an idea on how to achieve the basic objective of killing the game he points his shotgun at in a day's hunting.

Wing shooting with a shotgun is not difficult. It has been *made* to seem so (as has fly casting or hitting with a long iron out of a tight lie in golf), but when considered in terms of the actual number of individual movements, and of the various compensations one must make to hit a flying target, it isn't as hard as it is said to be. It's a *learned* reaction rather than a natural one. It requires as much practice to hit a flying target as it does to hit a baseball or a tennis ball.

Faced as I was with a maze of information and misinformation about the fundamentals of shotgun shooting, I decided—some ten years ago—to consult my peers, the men who write about guns and gunning as their way of life. The answers I received to my questions were as diverse as the personalities of the men who gave them to me. Here are a few statements as examples:

1. A shotgun is semi-aimed; has to be.
2. Lead is always computed by target size rather than by feet and inches.
3. Any man who shoots a shotgun bored less than modified (approximately 60 percent of the pattern hitting a 30-inch circle at 40 yards) and full choke (in excess of 70 percent of the pattern hitting the circle at the same range) is a fool and a game crippler.[1]
4. Heavy shot is the answer. . . . I never use less than #5's.
5. To hit a target, a man must know how far it is away from him, its direction of flight and its speed of flight. Without these answers, he will miss.

After a year, I quit asking questions and began thinking.

The service of our country taught me one thing if it taught me nothing else: an inherent hatred of lining up to do anything. I would never see the finest movie in the world if I had to stand in line to get in. The armed services, across the board, specialize in ultraconfusion and oversimplifica-

[1] For a discussion of choke, please see pages 37–39 and 74–75.

tion. Their terminology, for anything, must explain everything to the *n*th degree. As a result, a service shooting manual is a parody of instruction at best. It defines the simplest procedure, say, holding a shotgun, by a set of gobbledegook terms that it would defy a mathematician to unravel. Unfortunately, far too many of our shots who also write about shooting have not forgotten their service experience. The fact that you are firing a "Training weapon, shotgun, 12-gauge, semiautomatic, skeet adjusted" means nothing to a housewife who would love to learn how to shoot well enough so that Daddy would take her out at least twice a season in defense of "togetherness."

This, therefore, is a shooting book that will go all out to dispel the mystery of shooting. What it will teach is that foot position, hand position, head position, choke, stance, elbows—all the attendant garbage that is taught today—do not mean one bloody thing so long as you know what you are doing when you slap a shotgun trigger. I won't teach you to be an Olympic shot, but when you get through disagreeing with me and put into practice what I shall tell you, you will start hitting things with a shotgun.

After all, that's why you're reading this.

2 | SHOTGUN FIT AND SELECTION

Like learning to swim with a scuba outfit before you can stay afloat on the surface, buying a shotgun without knowing how to use one lays you wide open to being taken. You're the rube in the floating crap game, the pigeon a carnival barker searches out in the crowd around his display. Yet, for some strange reason, men who will invest their money carefully in blue-chip securities, make business decisions based on pure logic and facts, and drive a car all their lives without an accident, will decide, on the spur of the moment, that hunting is what they have been missing. First they buy a shotgun . . . then they try to learn to shoot. The cart before the horse.

If there is one necessity in the sport of firing a scattergun, it is that of gun fit. The relationship between gun and gunner is closer in some respects than that which exists between man and wife. A shotgun is an inflexible instrument that can perform only according to its construction, regardless of how you pretty it or lavish care upon it. Hence, Rule One: To shoot a shotgun well, you must have one that fits you.

I have read volumes written about the controversial subject of gun fit. Perhaps the most thorough of these tracts was written by Churchill, the famous English custom gunmaker. His work still stands as a classic in the field. But for some strange, almost unexplainable reason, both American and British authors are still prone to present the subject of gun fit as if it were a deadly and inscrutable enigma. Rather than make it clear, they tend to overburden the beginner with facts. I cannot, for the life of me, see that fitting a shotgun to *you* is all that difficult.

No two of us are built exactly the same. Physically, we all have separate characteristics that distinguish us from the herd. Some have fat faces, others thin. Some have high cheekbones, others low. I have a long neck; yours may be short. All these physical differences must be taken into considera-

PLATE 4. Custom-built and stocked to fit every physical idiosyncrasy, the author's Winchester Model 21, 20-gauge is typical of a fine tailored shotgun.

tion in choosing a shotgun to fit you. Just as a tailored suit, hand cut to a man's measurements, is bound to look better on him than a suit altered for him right off the rack, a tailored shotgun stock will enable you to shoot better. As in the case of the tailored suit, however, there are degrees of proficiency in tailoring. Not all gunsmiths are shotgun stock artists, any more than all portrait painters are Gainsboroughs. One thing all gunsmiths do have in common is their devotion to detail once detail is put together for them. Tell a gunsmith, who must be a craftsman of complete ability before he can truly qualify for the title, what you want, and he will be able to put it into wood for you. To do this, however, *you* must know what you want, and therein lies the rub.

To approach the subject of shooting theory in its fullest detail, you must first know the basic parts of a shotgun, be it semiautomatic, pump or double/over-and-under. Only then can you understand what your instructor is talking about when he uses the nomenclature of the parts of a shotgun. Should I speak of the "tang," you should know where it is and what purpose it serves. For that reason, it is mandatory that you commit Plate 5 to memory. Please bear with me on one point. Not all gun writers, admittedly, call gun parts by the same name. But if you learn the name of a gun part from me, you learn it as I have learned it from others; and inasmuch as I am the one who is to teach you to shoot the beasties accurately, let's do it my way.

A shotgun that fits you is nothing more (or less) than an extension of your arm. Your scatter-gun should fit your individual physique as precisely as your finger, which you should be able to point at an object without giving its aiming thought.

A number of factors in construction are involved in this process of ensuring that your gun is the proper fit for you personally. Before we go any further, it might be a good thing for us to dwell on the most common of these factors and define what they do in each case.

PITCH

Pitch in a shotgun is usually measured by standing the gun squarely on its butt plate against a wall. If the barrel lies flush with the wall, it can be

PLATE 5. Basic shotgun nomenclature.

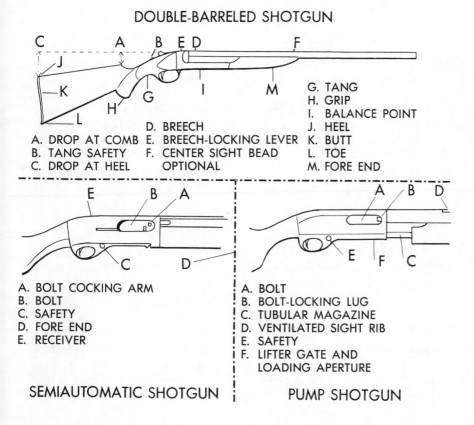

DOUBLE-BARRELED SHOTGUN

G. TANG
H. GRIP
I. BALANCE POINT
D. BREECH   J. HEEL
A. DROP AT COMB E. BREECH-LOCKING LEVER K. BUTT
B. TANG SAFETY   F. CENTER SIGHT BEAD   L. TOE
C. DROP AT HEEL   OPTIONAL   M. FORE END

A. BOLT COCKING ARM
B. BOLT
C. SAFETY
D. FORE END
E. RECEIVER

A. BOLT
B. BOLT-LOCKING LUG
C. TUBULAR MAGAZINE
D. VENTILATED SIGHT RIB
E. SAFETY
F. LIFTER GATE AND
   LOADING APERTURE

SEMIAUTOMATIC SHOTGUN

PUMP SHOTGUN

assumed that the gun has zero pitch. If the muzzle is 2 inches from the wall, the shotgun has a downward pitch of 2 inches. (This method of determining pitch is not entirely accurate; it will vary with barrel length. However, it is close enough for practical purposes.) Pitch affects the vertical placement of patterns.

DROP AT COMB

To simplify this measurement, lay a yardstick along the barrel of your shotgun and extend it rearward toward the stock butt. The distance (measured vertically) between the front of the stock comb and the yardstick constitutes drop at comb. This adjustment compensates for your neck length, the thickness of your features, and the height and placement of your cheekbones. Once more, this is a *vertical* control.

DROP AT HEEL

Using the extension of a line following the barrel of your shotgun rearward over the butt, drop at heel is measured by the vertical distance from the heel of the butt to this imaginary line. (See diagram.) Always classified in inches, this too is a *vertical* control.

❂   ❂   ❂

These are the major points with which you must deal when fitting a shotgun to your own particular set of physical characteristics. Stock length, which should vary from one individual to another according to the length of their arms and the shooting style they favor, must be taken into consideration as well. A good rule of thumb by which you may determine whether or not the length of your shotgun stock is correct for you is to do the following:

Place the butt plate of the shotgun in the hollow of your right elbow. Holding the gun vertical with your left hand, extend your right forearm along the stock with your trigger finger pointed. A shotgun stock that is *approximately* the correct length for you will allow you to crook the ball of your trigger finger over the trigger in this position. If your finger does not crook properly, either overlapping too far or not extending far enough over the trigger to give you a good feel, the stock should be altered.

The easiest method of lengthening a stock on a shotgun is to add a rubber recoil pad (along with wood insert shims if the pad alone is not enough to give desired length). I have yet to see the recoil pad, however, that will give you the even security of a solid butt plate on a shotgun. In my own case, I find they often slide out of proper shooting position at the shoulder

PLATE 6. To determine proper stock length, place shotgun butt in the hollow of your right elbow. A stock that is approximately the right length for you will allow your trigger finger to crook comfortably over the trigger.

on recoil, actually maximizing the recoil on a rapid second shot. Built in a series of cells or strata of composition rubber, they seldom react to recoil from one shot to the next in exactly the same manner. Rather, they tend to compress on one side, thus throwing the butt slightly out of position.

Your best bet on stock lengthening, this side of completely restocking the shotgun, is to have a gunsmith (or a competent woodcrafter) add a stock section or sections by lamination to gain the required length. These can be sanded and refinished to blend in harmoniously so that the appearance of the shotgun is not altered drastically. For consistent shooting results, you will find that a shotgun butt plate is far superior to any cushioning effect caused by a recoil pad.

A shotgun does not come to your shoulder in a straight line. Rather, the barrels and the stock are set at an off-angle to each other. The butt plate, furthermore, is of course shaped so that it will be applied evenly to your shoulder, allowing your eyes to fall naturally over the sighting plane of the

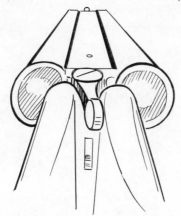

PLATE 7. How a double-barreled shotgun looks in shooting position when the comb is *far too high* for the shooter.

barrel or barrels. Pitch results from these factors. If the downward pitch is too great, you will find yourself shooting under most of your targets. Should the downward pitch be too slight, you will shoot *over* a majority of your birds. When you start missing straightaway birds, this is one of the first things you should check.

A very small adjustment of butt-plate pitch will make a tremendous difference not only in the pointing quality of your shotgun but also in recoil. As we shall discuss more fully later on, shotgun recoil becomes noticeable only when two conditions are present. If your gun does not fit you (and this particularly at the junction of the shoulder and butt plate), recoil gains in effect. The second reason for impressive recoil result lies more often than not in the method by which you are mounting your gun to fire. Let the butt be sloppily positioned because of poor mounting form, and you will feel its impact.

Books written a few decades ago gave, as standard, stock dimensions that differ radically from what we consider standard today. Before World War II, almost all shotgun combs were thin where your cheek met the wood—thin and low. Stocks were shorter by as much as an inch, and the drop at heel was dramatic. A shotgun of that era might have a stock 13¼ inches long, a drop at comb of over 2 inches, and a drop at heel of more than 3 inches. These measurements can be compared against what is considered to be a standard shotgun stock today, which has a length of 14¼ inches, a drop at comb of 1½ inches, and a drop at heel of 2½ inches.

Today's production guns do not deal in cast-on and cast-off. These two terms are best defined as follows:

Cast-on is the addition, or thickening, of the wood on the stock against which the shooter's cheek rests in full shooting position. This can also be accomplished by the gunmaker setting the stock in at an angle toward the shooter's face.

Cast-off represents the opposite of this—the thinning of the wood at the shooter's face, or the angling away of the stock from the action to the heel.

Shotguns that are available to us today have thicker combs by far than their predecessors, a thickness that allows the new shooter to find his spot on the comb as he places his face down to the wood that forces the eyes to center over the barrel. If you have a heavy face, you may have to shave off a bit of wood with a rasp and fine steel wool to bring the comb thickness into alignment for you; but this adjustment is a simple one that can be accomplished on the workbench in one evening.

Sitting in the gunrack of a close friend of mine is one of the old, original Parker shotguns, a double that in its heyday was considered a classic of the gunmaker's art. Who shot it at purchase is anyone's guess . . . how well he shot it would have to be a matter for discussion. He must have been built like a pigmy, for the dimensions of the stock defy imagination. The stock length on this masterpiece is 13 inches. The drop at comb is 1¾ inches, and the drop at heel takes a nosedive down to 3 inches. It looks like a demented pretzel. The pitch of this gunsmith's nightmare is fearsome, all resulting in a piece that could never have been shot either quickly or well.

Why this change in shotgun stocks over the years? Actually, there are two major reasons. First, we are bigger than our grandfathers, and often bigger in frame than our fathers. Being bigger, we need more stock length. Having longer necks, we need less drop at comb and heel. Though the second reason is obvious, it had to be pointed out to me by a man far more observant than I: We wear far less clothing when hunting than we used to before the lightweight, insulated garments so popular today were invented. These two basics, and constant research into shooting mechanics, have resulted in a production gun change that should make better shots of us all. It hasn't.

All hunters reach an age where they start worrying about the weight of the gun they are carrying. Where a 7½- to 8¼-pound shotgun never used to bother them before, they now start finding it too heavy to lug around the brush all day long. So they start shopping for a lightweight, *fast* shotgun. The two terms are never mentioned except together. For some obscure reason, men who have shot a gun that shades just off 8 pounds for years (and shot it moderately well) start tearing up the marketplace for a gun that will give them the same firepower at a weight that comes in a touch over 6 pounds. What they are doing is defeating the very premise around which gun agility is built.

Fast guns are balanced guns, not light guns. The fact that a shotgun weighs 7½ pounds has no bearing on how fast you can point it. If it is balanced—a shade barrel-heavy forward, with action weight centered between the hands and stock dimensions in good proportion—this gun can be

PLATE 8. The fastest gun a man can own is a balanced gun. With 28-inch barrels, and slightly barrel-heavy forward, this shotgun has excellent stock dimensions and weight.

pointed far faster than the ultralightweight toothpick that you found in some gun store 'way back on the shelf. To gain lightness in weight you must remove metal. If too much is taken off the barrels, the forward-throw balance of the piece vanishes. Such a gun may hop to firing position in a wink, but never in the same place twice. If the barrels are lightened, and, along with this, the action weight, you wind up with a toy that will point every way but right more often than not.

Some years ago, Winchester Arms, in a benighted moment of compassion for the tired hunters of the nation, brought forth (with much ado) their glass-barreled Model 59 Semi-Auto. Utilizing a metal sleeve around which they wrapped 500 miles of fiberglass thread, they turned out a shotgun barrel that had what they considered to be a new concept in gun balance. That was the understatement of the year. That barrel-light balance gave you the same pointing ability you could achieve shooting a baseball bat with the heavy end placed against your shoulder. It is now discontinued, and I don't believe it is missed by many.

Remember the mirror I talked about earlier? In addition to being an invaluable teaching aid in gun mounting, a mirror can also be a key factor in determining gun fit for you. Stand in front of a mirror, close your eyes tight, and then mount your shotgun as you would when you are firing. Once the gun is mounted, open your eyes and look down the barrel. Does your line of sight fall down over the receiver? Are you looking down the side or across the barrel? If you are, something is amiss, my friend. The gun does not fit you, and you will miss far more than you will hit with it unless you make some adjustment.

PLATE 9. Mounting a shotgun in front of a full-length mirror with your eyes closed, open your eyes after the shotgun is securely mounted, and check to see if your eyes fall directly over the sighting plane. By using this mirror method, your faults are instantly visible.

The sighting plane of a shotgun (the line along the gun that your eye follows to the target) should follow along the top of the receiver as well as along the barrel itself. All these, properly regarded, fall in line harmoniously, with no one factor standing out above the other. If this happens for you, you can be certain of two factors being correct—your *pitch* and *drop at comb* are correct.

If you have to pull the butt plate back against your shoulder and then position your face down to the comb, your *stock is too short*. If you have to reach a bit farther to bring the butt up past your armpit on mount, and then find you have to push your head forward to find a comfortable comb position, your *stock is too long*.

If you find that you are gazing down the left edge of the barrel or sighting plane, your *comb is too thick*. If you find your eyes coming into this same sighting plane from the right of center, your *comb is too thin*. If you find that your eyes are meeting the sighting plane well beyond the junction with the action, your *drop at comb is too little*. If you find your eye hitting the action where you must raise it to bring your line of sight into balance with the sighting plane, your *drop at comb is too severe*. (One point here: before doing any stock hacking at home, check the *pitch* at the butt plate first. It could be that your trouble lies there. Too much angle of pitch will produce the same effect as a severe drop at comb; too little will give you the same effect as having too little drop at comb.)

Some years ago my father had a severe tooth infection that spread into the sinus passages of his right cheek. During the corrective surgery that followed, the dental surgeon had to chip away part of the antrum to clear away the pocket of infection. After the wound had healed, Dad found that he had begun to miss straightaway birds consistently. Checking himself, he found that the operation had left a hollow in his mounting cheek that let his face come too far over the comb, resulting in a severe case of cross-firing. When he was lined up with the bird, his barrels were actually pointing to the *right* of where he was aiming. The simple addition of a homemade leather cheek pad on his pet gun made an instant improvement in his shooting.

You can adjust yourself to any shotgun you pick up if you give it the proper amount of thought and practice. My wife shoots a little Ithaca 20-gauge double that I carried for years and with which I killed a wagonload of game. The stock on that model would make a man accustomed to a fitted stock weep. For me, the drop was horrendous, and the comb, thin as a razor, had to be just barely touched with the face. Besides, the pitch was terrible and the stock was too short for me. But I learned to shoot that gun because I *had* to learn to shoot it—it was the only one I had. Yet when my wife took it over, the stock length was fine for her. By adding a comb-

PLATE 10. An example of what can be done to make a shotgun fit the shooter is this Ithaca 20-gauge double with a built-up comb pad and a rubber recoil pad on the butt, placed there after the angle of pitch had been radically altered.

building leather cheek pad and reducing the pitch drastically, we managed to turn it into a satisfactory field gun that she shoots well.

You are fairly safe in buying a new shotgun these days, a production model right off the rack. Stocked as they are in more or less standard dimensions, only slight adjustments will make them workable, usable buys that are well worth the money you pay. But beware of the man who would sell you a used gun that one of the boys brought back from France or Germany after World War II. These creations, while beautifully made (and priced), are stocked according to prewar principles, and without exception are difficult to learn to shoot.

Many of the Japanese shotguns being imported into this country today are made under the direct supervision of American key personnel in plants in Japan. These are often beautifully made firearms, faultless in both workmanship and design. Both Winchester and Charles Daly (to mention two outstanding manufacturers) are producing in Japanese factories firearms that would cost far more if they were made under the labor-market scale we have in this nation today. They are good buys at a fair price, and their stocking is such that only the slightest alterations are required in a majority of the models sold.

If you are going out to buy a shotgun, remember the check list. See to it that the gun fits you (or can be made to fit you with moderate adjustment) *before* you buy it, and you will find that your shooting troubles will be held to a minimum.

Once you have arrived at the point of understanding how a gun should fit you, your next problem is *what* shotgun to buy. For all intents and purposes, there are only three basic models of shotguns made today: the pump, or slide action; the semiautomatic; and the double, which has two barrels and is either of over-under or side-by-side design.

THE PUMP OR SLIDE ACTION

The whole firing cycle of a slide action is activated by the fore end of the gun. The shooter pulls the forearm toward his shoulder with his left hand after the round in the chamber has been fired. The action-thrust arm, a steel rod connecting the forearm and the bolt, rams the bolt to the rear as the forearm is pulled back.* As the bolt reaches the end of its travel, a fresh shell is raised on the lifter gate of the action to a position where the returning bolt face can engage it and ram it into the chamber. As the shell enters the chamber, the extractor claw grips its rim and the bolt locking lugs engage to hold the chamber closed during firing.

Pump action guns are usually fed from a tubular magazine that extends out through the forearm. Because many states forbid the use of more than three shells in pump (or semiautomatic) shotguns, a wooden or metal plug is usually inserted into the front of the magazine to restrict its capacity to two shells in reserve, one shell already having been loaded into the chamber of the gun. Perhaps the most popular of all shotgun models, pump guns are found wherever gunners gather.

THE SEMIAUTOMATIC ACTION

The semiautomatic (a shot being fired each time the trigger is pressed) is an action that depends on the energy generated by the discharge of a shell to activate it. Two methods of harnessing this energy are in use. In the more common one, a small amount of the gas formed by the burning powder is

* Some slide action guns have two action-thrust arms, one on each side of the magazine tube.

fed into a cylinder ahead of the chamber and below the barrel. The gas rams a small piston rearward and slams the bolt back. Most of today's semiautomatics use this gas-operation principle. There are still a few semi-automatic models being manufactured that use the direct recoil unlock of the bolt after the shell has been discharged in the chamber. Gas pressure, generated by burning powder, shoves the shell base against the bolt face, unlocking it to slam rearward against the pressure of the strong recoil spring.

The bolt on a semiautomatic shotgun, as we have seen, is driven rearward by the energy of recoil or expanding gas. A heavy spring within the action limits the speed at which the bolt travels. As the bolt reaches its extreme distance from the chamber, the fired case is ejected and the lifter gate raises another shell into position to be picked up by the returning bolt face. The extractor claw engages the shell rim, and the locking lugs twist into position to hold the bolt face against the shell in the mouth of the chamber.

Shooters have long noticed that semiautomatic actions, particularly the gas-operated ones, seem to kick less than pumps or doubles. Mathematically, this is not so; all guns of a given weight with a given load will have the same recoil. The kick felt by the shooter, however, is less with the autoloaders because the working of the gun's mechanism spreads the recoil out over a longer period of time; thus the acceleration against the shooter's shoulder is slower and he feels less of a thump. This helps to account for the autoloader's popularity with claybird shooters, who often fire hundreds of shots in a day.

THE DOUBLE BARRELS (OVER-UNDER OR SIDE-BY-SIDE)

These are what many feel are the safest of all shotgun actions. Inasmuch as the barrels and the receiver separate on a hinge when the breech-locking lever is pushed to one side, the shells are readily visible, thus enabling even a new gunner to tell whether or not his gun is loaded. Several important actions occur when this opening at the breech takes place.

(1) The discharged firing pins are recocked.
(2) In the case of a shotgun having selective, automatic ejectors, the fired shells are ejected from the chambers. If the ejectors are not automatic, the shells are merely lifted out to a point where they can easily be removed. (These ejectors, if automatic, are recocked with the shutting of the breech after reloading.)

(3) Some double-barrel shotguns have manual safeties, which must be moved to the "on" (nonfiring) or "off" (firing) position by the shooter. Others have automatic safeties which are moved into the "on" position by a mechanical hookup when the action is opened.

What the over-under and side-by-side doubles offer the gunner is instant choke selectivity. A single barrel gun has but one choke built into its barrel, but a double, of course, has one in each tube. In the side-by-side models, the open (or less choked) barrel lies to the right, with the tighter (or more heavily choked) barrel on the left. In the over-under models, the open barrel is on the bottom and the tighter barrel is on top.

Many doubles offer selectivity of barrels at shot, either through the use of two triggers (thus giving you an instantaneous choice of pulling the front trigger for the open barrel or the rear trigger for the tighter barrel) or through a barrel-selection device, either incorporated within the tang safety or a button on the top of a single trigger.

Over all, double-barreled shotguns are expensive when compared to the other two, often costing several times more at the base prices even in production models.

To select what you will need for your own personal kind of gunning, I feel it would be wise to consider a few factors that have heretofore been monumentally confused not only by the advertising copywriters but by the gun writers as well. Let's look at them in depth:

AGILITY

Contrary to popular misconception, the fastest gun for the man of average build to move into shooting position is one with a barrel 28 inches long. This statement is based on one vital point generally overlooked: a 28-inch barrel gives the shotgun that vital sense of weight-forward balance to counteract stock weight. As a result, it throws over and through to the target a split-second sooner than a shorter-barreled model would do under the same circumstances. This holds true in all three basic designs.

BALANCE AND FEEL

Of all the designs available, the over-under and the side-by-side possess the best overall weight balance in the field. The semiautomatics tend to be action and stock heavy because of their concentration of mechanism in the receiver housing and the stock interior. The repeater actions are a close second in that they have a feel of solidity that is found in the better-designed pumps.

SPEED OF FIRE

Speed of fire is a quality prized by hunters, although actually any multi-shell design can be fired as fast as necessary. Some early pump guns could be fired by keeping the trigger depressed and working the slide, but disconnectors in current models make this impossible. Even in the early days, it took a true expert with a pump to equal the autoloader's speed. A double is as fast as anything for two shots, even with the two-trigger models if the shooter is an expert.

SAFETIES

The thumb-operated top tang safety, which is the normal design on most double guns, is preferable to the finger-operated safety button in the trigger guard of most repeaters. It's not a question of time—either can be quickly disengaged while the gun is being lifted—but rather the ease of operation. It's just more natural to use the tang design.

RIBBED SHOTGUNS

A rib is a flat-piece of metal that runs along the top of a single barrel or over-under (or between the barrels of a side-by-side double). It serves to give the shooter a better sighting plane when he glances down the length of his shotgun. These ribs come in two general designs: flat and solid or raised and ventilated. Besides giving you a better sight picture, ribs—particularly the ventilated style—tend to disperse heat waves rising from a hot barrel.

I personally feel that you should learn to shoot with a shotgun that has all sighting equipment removed, but if you must have a sight bead, you are better off having the pair found on ribbed sighting-plane guns—the front and the center sight bead. These two beads virtually eliminate any possibility of cross-firing (that is, shooting to either side of your point of aim) on a straightaway target. The main advantage of a ribbed barrel is that it gives you the flat solidity of a pointing plane every time you glance down over it. When you think about it, that's quite a lot.

DEGREE OF CHOKE

Here is where the argument will never be settled. To my way of thinking, the perfect all-around gun is bored *skeet*, wide open, with almost no choke at all. It will give you even patterns through its entire range, patterns that will kill surely if you point it properly. It will also give you that depth of field that you need to kill a bird 8 yards or 35 yards from you without

PLATE 11. The Poly Choke is a device attached to single-barreled shotguns to allow the shooter a broad degree of choke selectivity.

worrying about blowing it to pieces. There are degrees here, however, that should be considered. You would never dream of getting into a duck or goose blind with a skeet gun, this aside from hunting decoying mallards that are to be shot at ranges of 20 to 30 yards. In waterfowl shooting, maximum choke is not only desired; it is both practical and humane. But for upland game and birds, a skeet boring will give you that degree of inclusivity that covers the vast majority of shots for you.

There is no such thing as an all-purpose shotgun. What might be a perfect gun for quail is not for pheasant. Many of us—and here I am no exception—shoot one shotgun at nearly everything we go afield for, but this does not mean that that particular gun is perfectly suited for the tasks to which we subject it. Properly (and expensively), a gunner should have a different firearm for each branch of the shotgun sports—upland shooting, plains shooting, field shooting and hummock or "hammock" shooting (i.e., in brushy patches found in the South), and for waterfowl. A few do possess the wherewithal to assemble such an expensive collection, but this does not assure them that they will shoot each of these shotguns with the same degree of skill as they might one or perhaps two.

The greatest advantage of the doubles is that they give a gunner a degree of choke selection that is not afforded the shooters of autoloaders or repeaters. As previously noted, a double usually has a different choke in each barrel, say skeet and improved cylinder or improved cylinder and modified, giving its handler an instant choice for chances at long or short range. The shooters of single-barreled guns must shoot with a barrel that would accommodate only one specific range well. The answer to this problem lies in installing on the single barrel a choking aid that will enable them to change the choke when they need to.

Perhaps the best known of these devices is the Poly Choke, a barrel attachment that works much like a hose nozzle. By turning it in or out, you can constrict or open the muzzle to give any degree of choke from full to wide open. Poly Chokes of current design have an integral muzzle brake to reduce recoil. The Poly Choke's major competitor in a crowded field is the Cutts Compensator, which gets the same results by a different method. The Cutts consists of a housing permanently fastened to the end of the barrel into which you screw tubes bored to any of the normal chokes. A slotted body vents escaping gases to act as a recoil reducer. The Cutts requires a small wrench for exchanging tubes, whereas the Poly Choke can be adjusted manually. Both designs work and both are popular with sportsmen.

The selection of a shotgun must lie in your own feeling of what you need, or, lacking this feeling, the faith you put in someone else's judgment of what your needs will be. Shotguns and their uses are as varied as the hunting areas in this country; if you plan on staying pretty much to one area rather than sampling them all, you should shoot the kind of gun that has become an approved standard there. It is not my intention here to tell you what to buy . . . only how to use it so that you can hit things with it when you fire it. With this in mind, let's get started.

3 | LEARNING TO POINT

Regard the index finger of your right hand. You would no sooner aim it at something than you would put catsup on ice cream. You might point it, but never aim it. That, in substance, is the crux of shotgun shooting: pointing, never aiming. A shotgun is nothing more than the extension of this finger, and pointing it requires no more coordination than it takes to point your finger.

Somewhere along the line, every new shooter begins to shut one eye when he shoulders a shotgun. For some strange and incomprehensible reason, he must feel that this makes him shoot more accurately. What it does do is exactly the opposite. By shutting one eye, you take away one very important factor, the sense of depth perception. Without this sense, it is difficult to estimate accurately range, speed and deflection. Whereas a rifle may be fired after a sighting process involving the shutting of one eye, a shotgun should be used with both eyes wide open.

No two of us see exactly the same; this one factor keeps in business eye doctors and laboratories specializing in glasses.

But one thing most of us have in common is a strong eye, called the "master" eye. One person may have it on the left side, another on the right. But this one eye will overpower the other when concentration of vision, such as in looking at one object as opposed to a number of objects, is required. The master eye will always dominate. In shooting, recognition of this master eye is all-important. Unless you know which is which, you start with a definite handicap.

In most cases, and I say "most" because there are notable exceptions, your master eye goes along with your master hand. Normally, a right-handed person will have a master right eye. *But not always!* To discover which of your eyes is master, take the following simple test:

With both eyes wide open, fix your sight on an object about 30 feet away. Holding this gaze fixed, point your right index finger at it with a fully extended arm. Once this is done, shut your left eye. If you have a master right eye, you should be looking directly over that index finger at the object. Now, check yourself. Open the left eye and close the right. The finger should now

PLATE 12.   Pointing his finger at an object 30 feet away, the author closes his left eye and looks over the extended finger at the object. Having a master right eye, his line of sight falls directly over this finger. If his left eye were the master, the line of sight would jump about a foot to the right. This simple test for determining the master eye is simple and time-saving. The subject is further clarified in the text.

be pointed about a foot to the right of the object. If the reverse happens, you have a master left eye and should become a left-handed shot.

Suppose you have a master left eye and still are right-handed? That is not an insurmountable problem, though it is a problem none the less. Here we must have a moderation of principle. While you would not shut the master left eye when you shoot a shotgun, you would have to squint it a shade to remove its dominance. If you cannot overpower it, you will cross-fire, day in, day out.

Eyesight, either corrected or natural, properly used, is the key to shooting success. You need not possess 20/20 vision to become a good shotgun shot. Many of the top guns in this nation today wear corrective glasses when they shoot. Rather you should have good eyesight, once again normal or corrected, at your disposal. Your eyes give you target recognition, deflection, speed, range—all the tangibles you must instantly assess to hit a moving object with a charge of shot.

Let's get back to pointing versus aiming once more. A shotgun is pointed for the simple reason that it does not possess the accurate sighting equipment of a rifle or a handgun. It uses a multiplicity of shot rather than a single round. It gives you spread of pattern to compensate for lack of fine accuracy. Even more important is the fact that you seldom have time to aim a shotgun when you are attempting to hit a bird rising and going away from you at high speed on a steep angle of deflection.

There is a pocket on your shoulder where the butt plate of a shotgun will snug-in comfortably every time you put it up. This pocket is formed by the heavy muscle at the base of your shoulder and the flat pectoral muscle on your right chest. The pocket lies directly under the right collarbone. Properly placed, a shotgun's butt plate will snug into this pocket without any conscious effort on your part to put it there. This is the one spot on your whole shoulder area where you can take the impact of recoil without any bad side effects.

Recoil is perhaps the new shooter's biggest bugaboo. It's a very complex subject, but for our purposes recoil can be defined as the rearward movement of the gun in reaction to the forward movement of the shot, shotcup/wad, and the products of combustion when a shell is fired. The movement is in accordance with Newton's law of motion which states that for every action there is an equal and opposite reaction. Because the gun is so much heavier than the forward-moving items, its rearward velocity is much less than theirs. Nevertheless, its kinetic energy, which is commonly termed "kick" when transmitted to the shooter's body, is considerable when a heavy hunting load is fired in a field-weight gun. Free recoil, which can be computed mathematically or measured experimentally, is about 18 foot

Shotgun Butt Placement

With right elbow held against his side, the author places his thumb into the butt pocket of his shoulder (PLATE 13, ABOVE LEFT). Placing the shotgun butt in the pocket, the author double-checks the placement and solidity of the butt (PLATE 14, ABOVE RIGHT). A close-up of proper butt placement with the shooting, or right, hand not in position shows the butt properly anchored in the butt pocket (PLATE 15, LEFT).

pounds for a 12-gauge express load. A shotgun held firmly against the shoulder, however, is not a free recoiling one, for some indeterminate part of the shooter's weight is added to that of the gun. Thus there is more mass than just the gun's to oppose the rearward movement, and the recoil never reaches its calculated peak. This is the reason why proper placement of the butt is stressed. A loosely held gun recoils freely, reaching maximum velocity and striking a sharp blow, whereas a gun seated firmly in the shoulder pocket, in effect, becomes part of the shooter and the kick is simply dissipated throughout the body.

The noise of a shot—or muzzle blast—adds a lot more to the recoil effect than most of us realize. In recent years almost all claybird shooters have taken to wearing ear protectors of some sort. These not only preserve one's sense of hearing but also prevent flinching and missed targets. Hunters rarely shoot enough to make ear protectors necessary in the field, but they help during practice.

Locating the exact spot on your shoulder to place the butt of your shotgun is a fairly uncomplicated procedure. The easiest way to do it is to extend your right hand away from your body as if you were shaking hands, leaving

PLATE 16. The blurring present in this picture is the result of 18 pounds of free recoil generated by a standard 12-gauge express load. With the shotgun butt held in proper position, even this much impact will not bother the shooter.

the elbow tight up against the hip. Now, raise the arm and hand back toward your shoulder, still holding the elbow against the hip. By extending your thumb, you should touch the shoulder *exactly* where your shotgun butt should fit when you mount it.

In 1964, in a book called *The Boy's Book of Gun Handling* (G. P. Putnam's Sons, $4.97), I introduced to a somewhat dubious shooting public a theory of shooting style called Contraflex. Stressing that this was relaxed shooting, a style designed to make one a competent shot with any firearm, I applied it to the rifle, pistol, and shotgun. What I accomplished with this was to remove the hodgepodge of "checks and locks" that so often accompany shooting instructions. Forget about your elbows, your feet . . . let them position at will. If you wish to crouch slightly in shooting, bless you. But follow two or three basics, and you'll never have to worry about where your round is going to wind up.

The theory behind Contraflex shooting lies in allowing the shooter to modify teaching axioms to his own particular style. Rather than have everyone holding a sporting arm the same way, a slight modification of principle to allow the shooter a greater degree of comfort is the key to accuracy with any gun. What Contraflex shooting does, without sacrificing style to any great degree, is to remove the pedantry from shooting instruction. In short, it makes shooting fun while still permitting no less thorough instruction.

Contraflex was originally conceived to alleviate recoil and the fear of it. Your body is a shooting platform; the gun is the cannon mounted in the turret. Just as a 16-inch gun aboard a battleship is mounted in a secure recoil mechanism, your shotgun should be the same. Your mechanism is as strong for its size as the springs and bolts in a turret.

Recoil is absorbed by the inertia of your body, particularly by the muscles of the abdomen. To be sure, the back and arm muscles do take up a share of the jolt, but the major part of the load is absorbed by your abdomen. The cushioning of the weapon on firing is taken up in the hold you have on it in the butt pocket formed at your shoulder. Thus, if you hold a shotgun properly, learning to do this so automatically that it becomes actually uncomfortable to do it any other way but the right way, then recoil becomes a barking dog that never bites.

Learning to mount a shotgun is the same as learning to hit a cut wedge shot in golf. The mechanics of the operation include a number of actions, all embodied in one fluid sweeping move that seems like a single motion. Broken down, it may seem to be a bit complicated, but the only way to learn to do it well is to examine the sequence of moves in their most basic parts,

PLATE 17. The left hand cups the fore end of the shotgun but never seizes it.

commit them to memory, and then practice until they become instinctive in execution. Knowing this, let's break down this mystique, this overtaught science that never seems to have the same meaning for any two people. In short, let's keep it simple.

We must consider the left arm and hand, the right hand and shoulder, the feet, the head and neck and, last, overall balance and foot position.

THE LEFT ARM AND HAND

The left side is your pointing side. With it you control barrel speed, deflection, elevation and depression of the weapon. I extend my left arm severely to give me a better sense of pointing feel. Yours should be extended *as far as it feels comfortable,* but never less than half. The left hand cups the fore end of the shotgun, but *never seizes it!* There must be moderation of control here to allow you the smooth swing that you need to stay with your target. Lay out your hand, palm up and with fingers slightly cupped. Now, drop the fore end into it and gently take hold. No more than that. The lighter your touch here, the better overall results you will get.

THE RIGHT HAND AND SHOULDER

The right hand clasps the stock just to the rear of the tang. This grip controls one thing only: it keeps the stock wedged solidly into the position on your shoulder. The right thumb (or forefinger in the case of most guns other than the double barrel models) is responsible for the release of the safety before it assumes its full·grip position. The index, or trigger, finger slides forward into the trigger guard and crooks the curve of the trigger. The hold of the last three fingers curled around the base of the grip is firm, exerting force rearward toward the shoulder.

The right shoulder is dropped *forward* and hunched slightly upward to form a pocket into which the butt plate is snugged. This movement, when done correctly, will cause the elbow of the right arm to flare slightly upward (Plate 19).

THE HEAD AND NECK

During the mounting process of a shotgun, the head falls *directly forward* to meet the rising comb of the stock. This movement will cause a pronounced

PLATE 18.   The right hand grasps the stock just to the rear of the tang, the trigger finger curving naturally into position inside the trigger guard.

PLATE 19. The right shoulder is dropped forward and hunched slightly upward to form the butt pocket.

forward extension of the neck. Your right cheek and cheekbone should fall toward the comb and meet it in the split second that the butt hits your shoulder. *Never* cock your head to the right or place your face on the stock *after* the butt is in position. Merely go to meet the comb as it comes to you. (See Plate 20.)

BALANCE AND FOOT POSITION

The easiest way I can think of to confuse a field shot is to make him start thinking about where his feet are when he is shooting. The feet assume an open stance, much as is used in a golf swing, *away* from the line of sight. Many teach that this angle should be 45 degrees. This tends to force you to face your target, making you better able to pick up its speed, deflection, and range. About all one can say is that you must be settled comfortably with weight evenly distributed on both feet and *forward* so that you have a sensation of having to spread your toes to keep your balance. Aside from this, your feet may be 20 or 5 inches apart, as you see fit. Just get the feeling of comfortable balance, and half the battle is won.

Though all these motions sound complicated now, they are actually a continuous sequence of events that follow one another in complete harmony. Let's see how it works.

Starting with the shotgun diagonally across your body with the stock downward and the barrel upward—that is, in a kind of low port-arms posi-

PLATE 20. In this slightly exaggerated position, you can see how the author's head has fallen directly forward over the comb to meet it as it arrives at the shoulder. Left arm extension, with the left hand cupped easily around the fore end, is comfortable, relaxed *Contraflex* shooting form.

Classical Gun Mount

PLATE 25 (ABOVE). The best place for daily practice to improve your gun-mounting style is in front of a picture mirror, thus giving yourself a series of constant visual checks.

tion (see Plate 21)—start your mounting motion. The left hand and arm swing the barrel and fore end up and *over* to the target. The left hand slides out the fore end into comfortable grip position. The right hand releases the safety, clasps the grip, and pulls the butt *up and rearward* into position at the shoulder. The body leans forward slightly at the waist, and your feet support your weight evenly. Your right shoulder (and your left as well, although not to the same degree) hunches *up and forward* to form the pocket where you are to bed the butt plate. Your head falls *forward* to meet the rising comb, and your eyes pick up the barrel as it settles through the line of sight between your eyes and the target. And that's all there is to it.

One thing, and one thing only, will make the procedure of mounting a shotgun come to you as an unconscious learned motion—practice. Not just handling the gun once a week, but studied daily practice. The best place for this, strangely enough, is in front of a mirror where you can observe your

The classical gun mount (*see facing page*) begins in a low port-arms position as illustrated in PLATE 21 (ABOVE LEFT). In PLATE 22 (ABOVE RIGHT) the left hand and arm swing the barrel and fore end up and over to the target. In PLATE 23 (BELOW LEFT) notice that the left hand and arm are at full extension. The right trigger finger is in the process of releasing the safety, while the eyes are still held in full concentration on the target. The upper body is bent forward slightly at the waist and the right shoulder has started its forward movement to form the butt pocket. Everything ready to go (PLATE 24, BELOW RIGHT), the author is in full gunpoint shooting position.

mistakes and progress. Keep a shotgun in your bedroom, or standing up in the corner of the downstairs closet—anywhere that it is convenient for you to pick it up and practice with it at least 15 minutes a day. If you have small children, impress upon them that touching the gun is strictly forbidden—and *enforce this rule!* However, if you have a son or a daughter who shows interest in guns, let them practice with you by using a toy or cut-down shotgun. Not only will your own proficiency gain, but their budding interest will be fanned by normal curiosity as to what Daddy is doing.

In the beginning, practice mounting the shotgun with no particular intention of picking out a target. Simply put it up, bring it down; put it up, bring it down. It will be dull at first. What practice isn't? But as your motion proficiency grows (and it will), you will find yourself striving to do better each time you follow the procedure. After a few days of dry practice, stop every now and then and perform the movement with both eyes shut. After the gun is mounted in the position that you feel is correct, open your eyes and check yourself. Both eyes should be directly over the sighting plane of the barrel. If they are, you are coming along well. . . . If not, you had better revise your form.

After a few days of practice mounting, begin picking out objects in the room at which you will point. Take the lower left edge of the picture on the far wall and see how close you can come to a perfect point at it. Now try the lamp at the other end . . . it's a rising bird . . . point it! When you do this, strive for one point of perfection. Though it will come slowly, it will come surely if you never relax your efforts. The gun is mounted without your looking at it. Rather, it simply appears at your shoulder and into your line of sight at the target. Fix your eyes on the target, and bring the gun up into position on it. Never remove your attention from the target, even for an instant, to check your position. If you are doing things correctly, the barrel will appear where it should be—on the bull's-eye.

You may have noted by now that all stress is placed on mounting the gun barrel up and stock down. There is a solid reason for this. Flying targets are *rising* when you start your mounting procedure. The simple act of bringing the barrel into the *up* position gives you a fine, near split-second edge to consider the tangibles we discussed before: range, deflection, and target speed. Mounting a shotgun barrel low is not only awkward; it also slows you down to the point of being clumsy. Throw your barrel up and through to the target where it settles in past the line of sight ready to point. By settling through the line of sight with the barrel, you have all the physical components of shooting—the gun, your eyesight, and your body—ready at your disposal.

After a period of practice, you will find that mounting a gun is becoming second nature to you. The fine art of having a barrel fall into position where it covers your target quickly is a joy to behold. You have it licked. Or do you? Can you do this standing on one foot? Can you straddle your favorite footstool and have an imaginary bird go up behind you and still cover him with ease? Can you lie flat on the floor, rise to a sitting position, and snap into a point? Can you do it with consummate ease while at rest in your favorite chair? You aren't sure? Let me tell you that this is not childish foolishness. Until you can mount a shotgun while nearly standing on your head, you have a long way to go. Back to the mirror, perfectionist!

One final point before we move along. Earlier, I brought up the fact that a shotgun does not possess the fine sighting equipment of a rifle or a handgun. That is why we must point it rather than aim it. While we have a front sight bead (and sometimes a center sight bead as well), we actually should never consciously see it. We *know* that it is there; our eyes and brain register its presence; but we do not consciously use it to point. This is the beauty of Contraflex—it allows you to shoot in one smooth, natural motion, without distracting thoughts of position and correction, but simply as you would point your finger at the target.

A charge of shot (never BB's or buckshot—just call it shot) covers a multitude of sins. At 30 yards, a skeet gun has a pattern as big as your front window. What matter if your barrel is off dead center on the target by as much as 6 inches? You will still have a large percentage of your pattern working for you. Therefore, precise aiming is not necessary. Not only is it not necessary; it is also downright time consuming. When a grouse is busting off through the trees at full flight, you simply do not have time to aim precisely. You snap up, point, and shoot—right now. If your lessons at home were diligently applied, the next sight you will see is a puff of feathers and a bird plummeting down in the arc of a good clean kill. And that's what this book is about.

4 | SWEEP SHOOTING

During World War II, I attended Naval Air Gunnery School at a base called Yellow Water, outside Jacksonville, Florida. There, in the short space of six or eight weeks, seasoned instructors were supposed to take keen-eyed but untrained and inexperienced young men and turn them into qualified (and deadly) turret gunners to man the Navy's patrol bombers. The mark of their success in this venture is that a fair number of our aircraft *did* survive the war . . . not as many as might have, but at least an encouraging number.

Teaching a healthy, ham-handed youngster, who consistently missed pheasant as a hunter prior to his service career, how to compute lead, deflection, and range through a machine-gun ring sight must have been a trying affair at best. One of the few things that I can remember from my training was a statement that an instructor used as an example. Roughly quoted, it went this way:

"Lead, as you will learn it, is to put yourself on the seat of a bicycle and ride down a sidewalk. Take out a newspaper from the carry rack, fold it, and then hit the front porch of a house you are passing without reducing speed. How far *ahead* of the porch you must hurl the folded newspaper is lead."

Concise, isn't it? Just lead the porch, and throw. But how far do you lead the porch? You can compute it if you know the speed of the bicycle, the distance the porch is from you, the size of the porch, the amount of wind that is blowing, the weight of the folded newspaper—they all add up to feet and inches plus trajectory of throw. If you try to do that with a flushing bird, he'll be in the next county before you figure out how far he is from you.

Lead, as we must apply it to shotgun shooting, is not a figure of feet and inches known in advance. It is the educated guess that you must make instantly and use on the basis of past experience. Because it is a guess, it can

PLATE 26. If you try to compute the three necessities of establishing lead by feet and inches (speed of target, target deflection, and target range), the bird will be in the next county before you arrive at a proper figure.

be only an approximation. To say that you lead a bird 15 feet is nothing more than a "guesstimate" at best. Therefore, to teach a student lead, to my way of thinking, at least, is to court disaster.

If we do not teach lead, then where do we start? The answer is simple: We borrow Mother's broom. A *broom?* That's right, because lead is going right out of your life and sweeping is going to take its place. Once you learn to sweep, your wing-shooting worries are past, and shooting will become a pleasure.

I first ran across sweep shooting when I was watching really good skeet

PLATE 27. Sweep shooting is the simple key to accuracy with a shotgun.

shots in action under tournament competition. To the man (and woman), they all performed the same basic action. After the bird had been shot, the shooters used an exaggerated follow-through with their shotgun barrels, swinging well past the broken target just to make certain that they wouldn't break the smooth fluidity of their lead swing. Curious, I asked a few of them why they did so. All maintained that they led the targets a certain number of feet and inches and that the only reason they followed through was to maintain swing to prevent barrel stoppage, which inevitably leads to shooting behind the target, the most heinous of all shotgun sins.

After I talked to these fine shots, I was greatly confused. Here I was, a medium-fair field shot at eighteen and a simply abominable skeet shot who had a hard time breaking 16 out of 25 birds each time I went to the club. I read and reread shotgun lead tables, as applied to skeet fields where the angles, speeds, and distances are always known. I still couldn't hit my hat with my hand. Suddenly, a great light dawned.

Knowing the speed of the target helps a person trying to hit it with a charge of shot. But what happens when you have to *estimate* the speed of your target? You make a calculated guess concerning its rate of passage; if you're wrong, you miss it a mile. But you shouldn't have to worry about speed any more than you should have to worry about deflection. That's the beauty of sweep shooting. You completely eliminate these two factors from consideration. The only thing that remains once these two constants are by-passed is range—and that, my friend, you cannot overlook.

Range estimation—call it depth perception, if you will—is the basic problem underlying most of our difficulties with a shotgun. It is amazing how few people can tell you exactly the distance they are from a given object when asked to do so. Many of them won't come within 15 feet of being right. Years of playing in golf tournaments has contributed much to my estimation of range. I can lay out 135 yards almost to the foot (the distance I can comfortably hit with a No. 7 iron). But range estimation of a flying bird, such as a pheasant, a grouse, a woodcock, a dove, must first come from basic target recognition.

Of all the waterfowl that fly, a Canada goose has more rounds of shotgun shells fired at him without effect than any other bird. I have seen sane and solid citizens rise up in a goose blind, scream *"Shoot!"* at the top of their voices, and blast away at a flight of honkers who are still 80 yards out from the decoys. In their eagerness they have forgotten that a goose measures a good 6 feet or more from tip to tip and that his body is a full 4 feet from nose to tail. Therefore, when he is near enough to look like, say, a decoying mallard, he is still way to hellangone out of shot-shell range.

As the result of a locker-room bet, two of my friends began carrying a tape measure with them on the golf course. The tape measure won them well over $300 during one golf season. My friends would ask a man who had just sunk a long putt how far he was from the cup. You'd be amazed to learn how an estimated 40-footer could shrink to its actual length of 23 feet when confronted with the implacable tape measure.

Range has only one relation to a charge of shot—the time it takes to reach its target. Within a second of time, a moving target proceeds another few inches or feet or yards. Therefore, if you know the range of your target, sweeping will down it for you every time. Now for the computation of range.

Let's say that the lot on which your house stands has a frontage of 75 feet, or 25 yards, on the street. Wouldn't you think that, after looking at this frontage daily from different angles, you could accurately judge a distance of 25 yards? Let's assume that you can. Now, knowing a given portion of a 40-yard range instantly (it's over 25 and less than 50), couldn't you say with relative accuracy that your bird is about 40 yards away as you swing on him? See what I mean? Acquiring a knowledge of approximate yardage isn't as hard as you think.

A few years ago I went hunting for mule deer in New Mexico. On the first day, my host killed a deer stone dead with one shot from his telescopic-sighted 250-3000. Turning to me with a grin, he asked me, "How far do you figure he is away from us?" Methodically, I started laying out seven iron shots down the face of the mountain, one after another. After doing so, I turned to him with a broad smile and said, "As best I can figure it, he's a tee shot and a wedge." The boy damn' near fell off the mountain, for his measurement of distance was still in feet and yards. Incidentally, the deer was 326 paces from where we stood—a comfortable tee shot and a wedge.

Sweep shooting begins with a radical approach, one that involves taping off the front sight of a shotgun. First, let's remove the temptation of

PLATE 28. Shotgun sights are not necessary in sweep shooting. You will do better if you either tape them off or remove them completely.

PLATE 29. To practice sweep shooting, tape a kitchen whisk broom to the barrel of a shotgun as shown at the left.

double-checking from the student. Next, tape a kitchen whisk broom to the barrel of your shotgun. Now, go back to what I mentioned before: Because a shotgun is not an instrument that we aim, why have sights? It is an instrument that we point, and that brings us back to the broom. Sweep shooting is exactly what it implies: the sweeping of your target out of the air with the barrel of the shotgun. Those skeet shooters I mentioned earlier were doing just that, even though they couldn't explain why or how they were doing it. Their exaggerated follow-through with their barrels was a kind of sweep shooting, although their approach to it was not. They were still thinking of lead in feet and inches. We will not.

To sweep a target from the air, we approach the target from the *rear* with the barrel. Once we have matched its course (deflection), we pick up its speed with the barrel. Now we are ready to sweep. With an increase in the speed of the barrel, we *pass* our target, maintaining its course as we do so, slap the trigger, and *sweep* the target out of the sky. Hence, the broom.

I have many neighbors who must regard me with the benign tolerance we extend toward someone who isn't quite right in the head. When I first perfected this approach to teaching shooting, I stood in our front yard, in full view of the road, and practiced mounting a kitchen broom, its long handle toward my shoulder and the broom end acting as the gun muzzle. As each little songbird flew by, I would sweep him from the sky with the broom, practicing as if I were using a shotgun and they were game birds. The results, at least on the part of the people viewing this performance, were amazing. The gas station attendant couldn't contain his curiosity: "What in hell were you doing with that broom the other day when my wife and I drove by? You looked like some kind of a nut or somethin'!" (It's a real good idea to practice sweep shooting in the *back* yard!)

Try showing up at a posh trap and skeet club, like the one I used to belong

PLATE 30. The best place to practice sweep shooting is in your own yard. Taking your practice shotgun with the whisk broom taped to the barrel, go out on the lawn and sweep each passing bird from the sky with the broom. Approaching your target from the rear, pick up its speed, sweep through it, and slap the trigger. That's all there is to it.

to in Long Island, with a kitchen broom lashed to the barrel of your favorite skeet automatic. I had trouble getting a squad together until I explained what I was trying to prove with the idea. Then *everybody* wanted to get into the act. Inasmuch as I have run across very few skeet shots who are good field shots (as I've mentioned, there are exceptions, but unfortunately not many), I had to sift a tremendous amount of misinformation to glean the wheat from the chaff.

The broom started paying dividends from No. 3 Station on, where the deflection angles start becoming severe. (For an explanation of the stations of a skeet field, see pages 91–92, 95–98. The No. 3 High House bird bounced into view. I peeked at it as I swung my broom by it, and then busted it to smithereens. No one was more surprised than I. Fascinated now (bear in mind that this was the first time I had tried this experiment), I proceeded around the field. The only bird I lost was at the No. 8 Low House, and that was caused by carelessness. I felt as if I'd just invented the wheel!

Though we have talked about mounting a shotgun until you must be sick to death of it by now, there is another term of which you will become even sicker before we are done. That term is "sweep." Your upper body is a gun turret; your lower body is the ship it stands on. The shotgun is the cannon, but it has to *sweep* to hit the target when you slap the trigger. To hit it, you must learn to pivot, just as well as you do in golf or tennis or skiing or what have you. Keeping your weight evenly centered and slightly forward, you turn at the waist and track your target with the barrel. This tracking motion must be smooth, for if it is jerky you defeat your own purpose.

One good way to learn how to pivot is so simple that it took me better than ten of my youthful years to learn it until Dad drummed it into my head. Why I never saw it myself I couldn't tell you, aside from the fact that I wasn't particularly observant at the time. But if we are to discuss basic rules —and all gun writers lay them down like the points in a sermon—these two will serve you in very good stead the rest of your days. Because a pivot starts with a shoulder turn, let's begin right there:

1. *On a pivot that swings to the left, lead the turn by pulling the barrel left with your left hand and shoulder.*
2. *On a pivot that swings to the right, lead the turn by pulling the barrel right with your right hand and shoulder.*

If you lead with a shoulder, your whole body will follow that lead. The barrel tracks just as it is meant to track, and everything works out just fine— with one small exception. How far away is your target? Getting back to range and estimation of range, you have a yardstick to follow here. If the bird is at maximum range, your pivot is slower than it would be if the bird was at minimum range. Your sweep stays the same; only your pivot changes. You still sweep him down with the barrel after you pick up his deflection and speed with the barrel; but your pivot has to maintain this deflection and speed, and it should be slower according to the distance away your target is when you fire at it.

PLATE 31. In the middle of a left-hand pivot, the author turns his body
at the waist (as you would in hitting a golf shot) and leads his pivot
with his left shoulder. If you lead with your shoulder, your whole body
will follow that lead.

When you learn to shoot a rifle, the first thing they tell you to do is to "squeeze" the trigger, not to yank it. Squeezing leads to precision—at least with a rifle. Squeezing is one thing that you must throw out the window when you are trying to hit a moving target with a charge of shot. The instant your target is ready to take, you take it—right away. If you wait for a breath exhalation and a squeeze to take place, all rhythm goes out the window, and chaos takes over.

A shotgun trigger is "slapped," a brisk down and rearward pressing that releases the firing pin to smack the primer cap of your shell. This slapping motion hasn't the slightest bearing on the accuracy of your fire; all it does is get it under way. The shot string (the entire charge of shot emerging from the barrel in a long string), all 9-plus feet of it, plus your sweep motion will take care of the hitting (or missing) very nicely. If your right-hand grip is firm in the rear three fingers (as it should be by now), slapping the trigger isn't going to vary the aim of the barrel by a hair.

Perhaps the most overused term in the history of wing shooting is that of "snap shooting." In essence, snap shooting is the discharge of a shotgun the instant the butt hits your shoulder, and it is referred to fondly by those who hunt woods birds—grouse, woodcock, quail in hummocks—*ad nauseam*. It is by far the most inaccurate method of shooting in practice today. The actual need for it is extremely slight.

As a youngster, I fancied myself as a lightning-fast shot. Though the hours I spent in practice made it possible for me to mount and fire a shotgun in a blur of motion, I seldom hit what I was shooting at. When I did hit it, I "shallumped" it—blew it to hellangone and beyond. My grouse were occasional gatherings acquired through the expenditure of countless shotgun shells. I was as fast as a cat, but the results were negligible.

Three of us used to hunt together . . . my dad, a man who now is in the upper echelon of a state conservation commission, and your author. Two of us used to vie for a bird when it hopped, blowing as many as four fast shots at it, only to have it fold with one decisive shot from Dad, who took the time to put his barrels on the bird before he fired. To me it was a humbling experience for years, until I learned that to hit things with a shotgun you have to have your barrels at least in the same county with your target.

Speed in shooting is important—in about one shot out of fifty! That shot may occur only once in the course of three hunting seasons, but when it does, and you *do* score, it is a lovely feeling indeed. But blinding speed of hand is not the key to accuracy. Actually, the reverse is true. The more you hurry your shot, the greater is your chance of missing, not only with the first shell but with successive shells thereafter. Then you stand there and watch a still-killable bird fly off unscathed. It is a hard lesson, but one that we must all learn. Overcoming speed is as important as acquiring it, but here moderation must be used.

Three years ago I had the extreme pleasure of working with two youngsters, both fifteen, who had the lovely sense of coordination of hand and eye that makes for a good wing shot. Blessed with the complete lack of fear that only the young seem to possess, and so imbued with confidence that "failure" seemed only a word in the dictionary, both had the ability to assimilate teaching rapidly—so rapidly that they passed even my own optimistic hopes. But the one thing that plagued them, and caused them to miss far oftener than their shooting form would indicate, was speed. After two weeks of solid work with them, I finally came up with an answer to their problem.

Taking them out to a trap field, I walked them down directly behind the trap house. One of the boys stepped up with his gun at ready. I took him firmly by the collar of his shirt at the rear, and whispered in his ear, "Now, I want you to tell yourself, out loud, 'Oh, look, there he goes' and then shoot." After I released the trap and sent a bird on its way, the first boy snapped up his shotgun, suddenly remembered what I had said to him, and recited the formula like a little gentleman. He broke the bird with consummate ease.

The next few days were spent reciting and practicing. Almost overnight the youngsters became the kind of shots that I felt they should—good, competent gun handlers who could fit in with any party for the rest of their hunting careers.

Such original teaching methods might not meet with the approval of some gunners, but it is a shame that they do not. That one sentence can save you a lot of grief. When the bird rises, look at him as you mount your gun, say loudly, "Oh, look, there he goes," and then flatten him. Your gunning companions may think you a bit demented, but they will be delighted with the results. On the spot, you will improve your hit/miss ratio by at least 75 percent.

Why do we miss straightaway birds? By this, I mean a bird that rises and flies directly away from the shooter. If your shotgun fits and you have the time, there is no reasonable excuse on the face of this earth for you not to kill every single straightaway you ever see the rest of your days afield—but you won't! You'll miss some of them just as sure as you are reading this sentence, but you will do so for one reason only—you stopped thinking!

Bear in mind a cardinal fault that seems to occur in almost all gunners: the failure to recognize that a straightaway bird is *still* a deflection shot, in respect to the angle of the line of fire from the shooter to the target. Because the bird is *rising* in flight, you miss him in one of two places—to the side or under him. You seldom, if ever, will shoot over him. Thus, by way of counteracting the theory of never aiming at a shotgun target, the straightaway is really an aimed shot. The barrel is carefully laid on the bird and then *raised* slightly to cover him just as you slap the trigger. Doing it this way, and taking your ever-loving sweet time, you'll kill every one you shoot at hereafter. Just cover and slap—that's all there is to it. Sound too easy? Let's take the reverse.

The easiest shot in a shotgun handler's book should be an incomer, that is, a bird that flies directly toward the shooter. Still a deflection shot, the incomer represents the simplest of all wing-shooting feats. Yet for some strange reason this is the shot most blown by supposedly fair gun hands. Once again, there is no excuse. An incomer is a deflection shot, the angle being computed by a swing through or sweep from the rear of the bird and past him to cover him as you slap. All you must do to hit an incoming target is to pick up its speed of arrival, swing through it with your sweep, and pass it so that your gun muzzle blanks it out when you slap the trigger. Take a peek around the barrel after the shot, and you'll see a bird on the way to the ground.

When we deal with truly fast targets, such as a twisting dove that has been shot at several times before it gets to you, or a Canada goose passing with a good wind on his stern, they demand long sweeps, not long leads. As mentioned before, you establish that a certain bird is going like the hammers of hell when you track him with your gun barrel. You know his deflection because you have followed his course. Now, you must exaggerate his speed when you pass him, seemingly to "overlead" him, if you will. Take my word for one thing here: In the course of a year, the number of birds that you shoot too far in front of will be more than outweighed by those you have left the charge far to the rear of. Let me give you a good example.

Several years ago I was duck shooting one late afternoon on the upper reaches of the Tamaze River, above Tampico, Mexico. The birds were coming mainly from behind us, sweeping in over a low bluff, and wheeling to pass downriver. After a few minutes of frenzied shooting, three pintail, all in a line and about six feet apart, buzzed in over the bluff, headed for the far side of the river. Pivoting fast, I swept through the lead bird and slapped the trigger—only to kill the *third* bird stone dead! My guide slapped me on the shoulder and told me what a fine shot I was, while I stood there absolutely unnerved. I knew in my own mind that the sight picture I had in my brain had looked correct. What I did not know then was that I had not given the bird a full sweep, an exaggerated laying through of the muzzle needed to compensate not only for his speed of passage but also for the velocity of the wind at his rear, which added considerably to the speed of his passage.

You will seldom need an oversweep, but it is a good thing to use when you find yourself missing targets you felt you were on when you touched off the shot. Whitewing doves, perhaps the most deceptive of all wing-shooting tar-

PLATE 32. With an exaggerated sweeping through of the gun barrel, the author "oversweeps" a fast incoming target to ensure that the shot charge stays well out in front.

gets, inasmuch as their speed of flight is not immediately taken into consideration, are one species that demand an oversweep. Flaring jacksnipe, startled teal—all these take that little bit extra to score when you very easily can miss. Just a point to remember.

Sweep shooting, as we have discussed it here, is one of the major reasons that this book was written. While not a universally recognized teaching method, sweeping allows a new shooter to hit flying targets much faster in the course of his training. It can be summed up in one sentence, one that I recommend you to commit to memory:

Place the barrel behind the target; track through it to pick up its speed and deflection angle, and slap the trigger as the barrel passes the target in an even sweep.

It is just that simple.

5 | LOADS AND THE PELLET SHOCK THEORY

The number of shotgun shells expended in America annually is staggering. No one knows the exact total, but it is known that *over a half billion shells* were fired at registered Amateur Trapshooting Association targets alone in a recent year. How many were fired in practice, at skeet, and by the country's 20 million-plus hunters is anybody's guess. Probably a couple of billion. In muzzle-loader days, everyone loaded each shot himself, of course, and many hunters reloaded their shells (replaced the primer, powder, wads and shot in a fired case) in early breech-loader days. This practice largely died out in the period between the two world wars, except with experimentally minded gun cranks, but again attracted widespread interest following World War II. Now millions of shooters reload almost all of their shells, and one of the reasons for this is that each of these men has a definite, unshakable faith in his own ability to pick the best load for his kind of shooting. *Yet it's doubtful if any one of them completely agrees with the next!*

A quick glance at the shell listings in a major catalogue put out by, say, Winchester Arms, reveals shot-shell loadings until you wonder why in the world anyone would need such diversification. From buckshot and BB combinations to high-speed express No. 9's, the list is dramatic—but quite unnecessary. For example, there is nothing in the world that a charge of No. 9's will do that a charge of No. 7½'s won't do better, with the exception of the saturation patterns needed for woodcock; and to use a load of No. 4's when you have No. 6's at your disposal is folly. About the only use for No. 2 is for geese, and here No. 4 will do every bit as good a job.

Back in the mid-1940s, Dad and I started investigating an idea that had plagued both of us for some time. We felt then that the multiplicity of shot striking a target had much more to do with the shot's ability to kill than did its size. It seemed reasonable that living tissue struck many times by small

Standard Shot Chart

No.	12	11	10	9	8	7½	6	5	4	2
DIAMETER IN INCHES	.05	.06	.07	.08	.09	.095	.11	.12	.13	.15
APPROXIMATE NUMBER OF PELLETS TO THE OUNCE	2385	1380	870	585	410	350	225	170	135	90

	Air Rifle	BB	No.4 Buck	No.3 Buck	No.1 Buck	No.0 Buck	No.00
DIAMETER IN INCHES	.175	.18	.24	.25	.30	.32	.33
	NUMBER TO THE OUNCE		APPROXIMATE NUMBER TO THE POUND				
	55	50	340	300	175	145	130

PLATE 33. Standard Shot Chart. These are the actual sizes of the shot pellets in a shot shell. No. 12 is "dust" shot. No. 00 is buckshot for deer. (*Courtesy of Olin Mathieson Chemical Corporation*)

shot would be hit harder than would the same tissue struck by fewer and heavier objects.

Before civilization reached its present flowering, and before dreams of urban expansion grew within the bosoms of the founding fathers of the country town of Milton, Pennsylvania, some half million crows wintered there every year. They would roost on an island in the middle of the Susquehanna River, which runs right down through the town, parallel with the main street, by the hundreds of thousands, screaming and raising eight kinds of hell each night. Not many people wasted any time or shells to eradicate them. After all, they had been there every winter since people could remember. But there

PLATE 34. The Promised Land.

were three people—three wild-eyed, dedicated screwballs like me and two of my friends—for whom this was the Promised Land. Where else could you secure limitless shooting four months of the year?

Bert Popowski, sage of the black bandits, crow expert extraordinary, wrote a book called *Crow Shooting* that the three of us had almost memorized. We tuned crow calls and practiced with them until we could fake out a flight of birds almost as well as the expert from whom we had learned. That copy is in my bookcase now—dogeared, thumbed, underlined, and read and re-read many times. We literally lived and slept crows and the shooting thereof. For the testing of the theory of multiple pellets versus larger pellets, we had a built-in laboratory.

Just after we returned from service, there occurred a big, destructive flood in Williamsport. This flood, as had all its predecessors, filled the basement of one of our local sporting-goods stores, wetting down cases of shotgun shells that had been left to shift for themselves in the face of the rising water. Not all of the shells were ruined, and the price the store owner asked for the damaged hulls was more than reasonable. To be sure, not all of them fired—many were so swollen that they would not even slip into the chamber. But in the main they worked well enough. When you realize that we were going through 30-odd cases of shotgun shells a winter, you will understand that the cost could have been monumental.

My mother, bless her soul, would accept as dinner guests (at the kitchen table, not in the dining room) three wet, cold, muddy boys, all talking at the same time, at an hour that would make a hired cook quit in disgust. After eating everything in the house, we would troop out to our cars and bring in specimen crows for autopsy. There, on the same kitchen table, we would carefully defeather and probe each cadaver with the dedicated curiosity of medical students. Each shot hole was traced from entrance to end, taking in every organ it struck and the angle at which it was struck. We recorded hemorrhage and tissue damage, bone destruction—everything that made something alive dead. We learned more than we ever bargained for when we started the project.

A crow is a tough bird to kill. He must be struck hard to hammer him out of the air dead on contact with the ground. So, for that matter, are ruffed grouse, wild turkey, geese, and pheasant. The quail, doves and shore birds are much easier to down in their tracks, and with less punishment. After all our autopsies, some truly amazing facts came to light:

1. Only one bird out of six was struck in the heart or the pericardial sac surrounding the heart.
2. About one out of four birds was hit in the lungs or lung cavity.

PLATE 35. Those evenings spent autopsying dead crows on the kitchen table revealed much about pellet shock.

3. Shot damage to major blood vessels was occasional.

4. In many instances, intestines, liver, and the lower bowel were the only organs struck, this attendant with bone damage *not* including the backbone or the nervous system therein.

5. In every case of multiple-pellet entrance, there was extensive contusion evident. Yet with large pellet entrance, there was heavy local tissue damage but only moderate evidence of contusion.

In many cases, the only thing we could see that the bird could have died from was sheer fright!

Have you ever been startled, actually scared out of your wits by a sound or a sight? You will remember that there was a sensation like a hammer blow in the pit of your stomach, a feeling of tingling all over your body. This was nothing more than a massive nervous-system impulse triggered by a startled brain that alerted every nerve fiber in your being. The same effect can be seen by dropping a stone into a puddle—the waves spreading out from the impact area are the result of shock, a reaction to an action. The same would apply after an earthquake or a heavy blow. All of these generate shock, a shock that does not contain itself within the area of generation but spreads throughout the stricken object.

After we learned that a body can die when struck with sufficient force in a nonvital spot, we asked how this could occur. It was then that we hit the stone wall of lack of knowledge concerning the nature of shock itself. Doctors I have questioned intensively on this subject are in universal agreement on but one point: there is a definite correlation between shock and the displacement or disruption of the function of the capillary bed, that hair-fine network of blood vessels that brings life and nourishment to living tissue. This would agree with our nonmedical "autopsies" of dead birds. In every case of multiple-pellet strike inflicting death without damage to a vital organ, we found extensive areas of contusion—contusion brought on by the effect of a multiplied blow to the capillary bed in that area of the bird's body.

After research that worked backward from a known reaction to a probable cause, we evolved a formula of sorts, but one that cannot be proved any more than can the theory of life itself springing from the sea. We drew the conclusion that multiple shock from the impact of many small, rather than a few large, pellets seemed to bring on a quicker, more violent death than the results of the impact of heavier pellets in smaller amounts. We judged pellet shock to be roughly the *square* of the number of pellets striking living tissue. The impact of 12 pellets would give a pellet-shock ratio of 144, whereas 3 pellets striking the same place would bring about an impact of only 9. So where does this leave us? I'll tell you—right up a tree hanging by our tails.

If the hours I have spent arguing theory had been spent in the diligent pursuit of coin of the realm, I would be a rich man today. For that matter, the time I have exhausted learning to hit a driver off a fairway lie would probably have put ten shares of General Motors in my stock account. But all our theorizing boils down to one fact: Small shot kills hell out of game birds if used in proper perspective, within a working range of 40 yards or less.

Until a few years ago, a majority of the shooting preserves, those pay-as-you-kill game farms that allow you to pursue the sport of shooting well past the confines of the regular season, had definite policies concerning shot sizes. The preserve owners usually restricted you to shot sizes no smaller than No. 6, figuring that their cripple loss would be reduced. In fact, it was not reduced; in some cases it was increased by this insistence that large shot would kill rather than cripple.

A shotgun pattern, from a gun choked full, is supposed to show a 70 percent or better impact within a circle 30 inches across at 40 yards. Taking this as a norm, we know that while a charge of 6's is usually going to show about the same pattern percentage as a charge of 8's, there will be many

PLATE 36. The tremendous slamming shock to the bird's nervous system is far greater when he is hit by many small pellets rather than by a few large pellets.

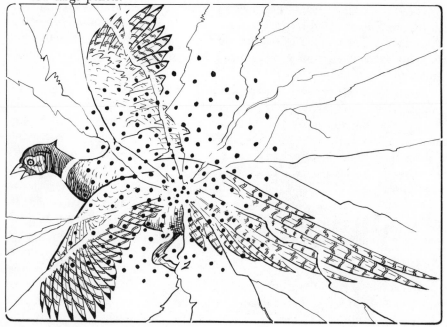

more 8's in this same circle than 6's. One other factor has a definite effect here as well. No shotgun pattern is absolutely uniform in scope; all have holes and concentrations. A bird is far more likely to be struck by fewer pellets with a charge of heavy shot than he would be if fired at by the same weight charge made up of smaller shot. All these add up as obvious plus entries on the ledger, but what of the one not so obvious entry that we all should make? When a bird is struck with but a few pellets of small shot, it does not mean that the bird must be crippled or die from its effect. Large shot, with the individual tissue damage found at each entrance and exit hole, has a far greater crippling potential.

The use of small shot has some negative aspects as well. Small shot tends to dissipate its force far more rapidly than heavy shot, inasmuch as it does not have the weight to keep it going over long distances. Being light, it tends to wander after a certain point. Knowing that its effect is limited, to be practical, to a range of 35 yards, small shot makes a perfect first-shot load on flushing birds. It is absolutely worthless as a load for prairie pheasants or passing ducks. There is a point where moderation must take the place of enthusiasm.

At the risk of sounding egotistical, which is not my intention, I like to use small shot because it allows me a pattern saturation on quartering birds, which I usually try to shoot in the head and neck rather than in the body. This offers me the constant of a clean slapped-down kill rather than a half-dead, possibly crippled bird. Not nearly so hard to do as you might assume it would be, head shooting requires just that fine edge of regular practice to keep in the rhythm of your swing. When you shoot a lot, you can head shoot with reasonable regularity.

Throughout this text we have mentioned "choke" in shotgun boring from time to time. Perhaps it might be a good idea to define "choke" in depth. Choke in a shotgun barrel is a constriction that makes the shot charge behave like the water flowing through the nozzle of a garden hose: the tighter the nozzle is constricted, up to a point, the finer the stream. Over-constriction causes patterns to disintegrate.

Despite the choke designation stamped on the barrel, the only way to be reasonably sure what a given load will do in a given barrel is to shoot it. Chokes of hunting guns are determined by measuring the percentage of pellets in a shot charge which strike within a 30-inch circle at a range of 40 yards. Accepted terms for the common borings are: "cylinder," which gives about 40 percent patterns; "improved cylinder," 50 percent; "modified," 60 percent; and "full," 70 percent or greater. (Skeet guns are often patterned at 30 yards rather than 40, as they are normally used only at short range. "Skeet #1" boring averages about 40 percent at 40 yards, and

"Skeet #2" about 50 percent; thus these chokes are equivalent to the hunter's "cylinder" and "improved cylinder" borings.) Occasionally such terms as "improved modified" and "superfull" are heard, the former taken to mean 65 percent boring, the latter anything significantly above the 70 percent of the common full choke.

Modern ammunition has changed our thinking considerably concerning choke in today's shotguns. The biggest of all these breakthroughs would have to be the incorporation of the pie crimp at the end of a paper (or plastic) shot shell. A pie crimp looks exactly as you would imagine it would look—a pie cut into 6 or 8 sections. When the shell is fired, these sections blossom open like a flower, allowing for clean passage of the shot down the barrel. Old shells had a top wad with the end paper of the shell crimped down around it. When the shell was fired, the wad went out the barrel ahead of the shot charge, often causing openings, or "holes," in the pattern of shot at the target. Pie crimping eliminated this hazard overnight, but it served to point up the need for another, and equally important, development.

Bugaboo of the arms makers for years was a factor called "pellet deformation." When a column of shot progresses the length of a shotgun barrel, the pellets that touch the side of the barrel are flattened, sending them through the muzzle in a shape that is no longer round for accurate passage through the atmosphere. Obviously, if those pellets could be shielded, the entire shot charge would be made that much more accurate.

The two major arms makers in the United States attacked the problem separately. Both of them brought out answers to the problem the same year: Winchester with the Mark 5 shot shell, and Remington with its revolutionary "ram wad."

The Mark 5 shot shell incorporated a sleeve of plastic, more properly, a wrapping of this material, around the entire shot charge. This wrapping remained with the shot column all the way out the barrel, opening and falling harmlessly behind the shot as it reached open air. Test results were amazing in this model, showing that shot could be contained and still be even better in accuracy.

Remington's innovation was a base wad of plastic (placed just ahead of the powder charge in the shell) that had a shot cup in the top end. This cup held the entire shot charge. Made of much thinner material than the base of the ram, the cup was sliced lengthwise at four places equidistant around its perimeter. When the shot emerged from the muzzle, air action against these slits caused the wad to fall off to the rear and allow the shot to continue unimpeded.

These two shells were greeted with acclaim throughout the shotgun field. They had accomplished what no one ever dreamed could be done. They had broken, wide open and forever, the bugaboo of shot fallout due to deformation. Not only did they deliver comparatively even patterns; they also delivered a higher percentage than they were supposed to under *all* borings. In short, the gunner using these shells stepped up his choke one position, if not two in some models.

Let's get back to the statement I made earlier about the effectiveness of skeet boring as opposed to tighter-choked shotguns. Today's ammunition, with it's combination shotcup/wad column of plastic and its pie crimp, gives extremely uniform patterns compared with shells of just a few decades ago. Most of the pellet distortion resulting from shot/bore friction has been eliminated, as have the blown patterns caused by the old overshot wad. A skeet bore will give you an even distribution of shot throughout the impact pattern that is as important as a concentration. It has always been my feeling that shot distribution is as much a key to shooting success as is good gun pointing. A skeet-bored shotgun will give you all the choke you need for a great majority of the shotgun wing shooting you do anywhere in this great country of ours. I have used, successfully, a skeet double 12-gauge on South Dakota pheasants, combining this open gun with the extra power of plastic-sleeved No. 6's. With it, I could make the 40- and 45-yard kills you are required to make to score in this wide-open shooting country.

There are limits to small shot, limits imposed by the hunter's preference for decent table fare. A bird *body hit* at normal range with a load of No. 9 shot is fairly well riddled. If you hit him in the head and shoulders, that is something else entirely. But taking flushing birds (and rabbits for that matter) inside normal ranges, some will prefer to use No. 8 or even No. 7½ shot to reduce the amount of lead in a Sunday dinner. Not that No. 9 shot will not do the job for you—if anything, they do it a bit too well. The slamming impact of a charge of 9's on a bird is obvious to the eye. The head jerks rearward; the wings break; the body puffs feathers. Just as if you had reached out and struck your target with a gigantic hammer, it is completely dead in an instant. For a clean, humane kill, small shot has no peer.

Shock acts in many ways on living tissue. As I mentioned before, the disruption of function of the capillary bed does not stop at the impact area. There seems to be a definite breakdown throughout the whole system; "pooling" might be a better term for it. Nerves are jammed and compressed; blood stops flowing; the brain is struck a hammer blow of impulse—and all without regard to the number of organs that are affected by actual impact of shot. I learned about shock the hard way.

In the mid-1950s, my father and I joined a friend of ours on a then annual shooting trip after sora rail in the Patuxent Marsh below Baltimore, Maryland. The marsh is covered with wild oats; high, reedy cover that shields not only the quarry but the gunners as well. You hunt from a punt, a shallow-draft boat that is propelled over the marsh at high tide by a pusher using a 16-foot push pole. As he heaves you through the high oats, you stand astraddle the bow seat, bracing yourself with your legs and knees as you peer ahead for flushing birds. It is fascinating hunting.

As a safety precaution, all the pushers whoop from time to time to give their counterparts in the marsh their position to avoid stray shot and shell drifting in your direction. On this particular day, Dad and I started off in separate boats side by side; then our pushers, working with a singleness of purpose caused by the daily bet as to who pushes "high gun" on a tide, separated and went their own ways. In this process, we worked in a swinging curve, finally winding up with our craft about 50 yards directly in front of Dad's boat. Naturally, he could not see me any more than I could see him. My pusher seemed loath to whoop, so I entered the race, emitting startling yelps from time to time to ensure safety of life and limb. Perhaps I became interested in the shooting and forgot to yelp. I don't remember.

I weigh 180 pounds and stand almost 6 feet in my stockings. I was braced solidly across that bow seat. I felt myself hit a gigantic blow across the back; then dully I could hear the crack of Dad's 20-gauge as I fell straight forward into the marsh. My head roared; my back felt as if I had been swatted with a baseball bat. Numb, I crawled back into the boat, unloaded my shotgun, and sat there dazed. After a few moments, I slipped off my poplin safari cloth shooting jacket, under which I was wearing a wool sweater and a khaki shirt. There, tattooed on the cloth of the back, was the whole story. Twenty-eight No. 9 pellets had centered on me, all striking full on the back of my jacket. Seven had penetrated my sweater; one had sifted through my shirt to stick into the skin. Though the tall reeds had filtered a majority of the wallop out of the shot charge, the massive blow those infinitesimal bits of lead had dealt me really impressed me with their power. Had we been 15 yards closer, I doubt if I would be writing this today. As it turned out, I had 28 black-and-blue bruises on my back the next morning. I *know* how hard small shot hits.

It is all very easy to recommend what shot to use for this and that. I have read shot tables, disagreed with most of them out of hand, and then sworn that someday I would sit down and figure out what I would use under all given circumstances. The recommendations in the list on page 78 are not meant to be absolutely rigid, but simply represent my individual preferences.

As you go over the list, you will note that there is a pattern to my own feelings as to shot and shotgun sizes. This is one I have set up over the years, as you may have in your own shooting. What I am looking for is maximum pattern and shot disbursement on close-range shooting, and maximum striking power when I start dealing with targets out at the long ranges. You *can* kill a decoying mallard stone dead with a load of No. 9's if he gets in tight over the decoys, but you will do it better with No. 7½ express day in,

Species	Type of Shooting	Minimum Shotgun Size	Minimum Shot Size
Puddle ducks	jump [1]	20-gauge	No. 7½ express
Puddle ducks	decoying [2]	20-gauge	No. 7½ express
Puddle ducks	passing [3]	12-gauge	No. 6 express
Diver ducks	passing	12-gauge	No. 6 express
Diver ducks	decoying	20-gauge	No. 7½ express
Pheasant	driven [4]	12-gauge	No. 7½ express
Pheasant	flushing [5]	20-gauge	No. 8 field
Woodcock	flushing	20-gauge	No. 9 field
Mourning dove	passing	20-gauge	No. 8 field
Mourning dove	flushing	20-gauge	No. 8 field
Whitewing dove	passing	20-gauge	No. 7½ field
Geese	passing	12-gauge	No. 4 magnum
Geese	decoying	12-gauge	No. 6 magnum
Desert quail	flushing	12-gauge	No. 7½ field
Chukkar partridge	flushing	20-gauge	No. 7½ field
Ruffed grouse	flushing	20-gauge	No. 8 field
Wild turkey	normal	12-gauge	No. 6 express
Clapper rail	flushing	20-gauge	No. 8 field
Sora rail	flushing	20-gauge	No. 9 field
Jacksnipe	flushing	20-gauge	No. 9 field
Sea ducks and coot	decoying	12-gauge	No. 6 express
Sea ducks and coot	passing	12-gauge	No. 6 magnum
Bobwhite quail	flushing	20-gauge	No. 8 field

[1] "Jump"—putting a bird to flight by dog or human proximity, but applied only to waterfowl and shore birds.

[2] "Decoying"—bringing a flock of ducks within shooting range through the use of plastic or wooden replicas of live birds.

[3] "Passing"—placing yourself in a position where you are shooting at birds bound from feed to water or the reverse.

[4] "Driven"—originating in Europe and the British Isles, this involves pushing to flight birds running on the ground, either by human beaters or dogs, so that they fly directly over a set of predetermined shooting stands. In this country, driven shoots are more properly release shoots, conducted on shooting preserves, where the birds are thrown in the air and allowed to fly over a set of guns stationed around the perimeter of the release area.

[5] "Flushing"—putting a bird to flight by dog or human proximity.

day out. All that a table like this can do for you is to point out the moderate approach to loadings rather than the extreme. While extremes will work, they fail too often to be of practical use.

Every shotgun has its own built-in "preference" for shot. Some barrels will shoot No. 7½'s in patterns that will make you weep for the beauty of them, and then turn around and spray No. 6's all over hell's half acre. The only way you can tell what your own gun "prefers" is to take the time and

PLATE 37. Using a stepladder while patterning a shotgun allows the shooter to offset the effect of recoil from an aimed shot.

trouble to pattern it in some pleasant afternoon. It is not difficult to do, and you will be well rewarded.

Set up a big sheet of wrapping paper on a wood frame at a distance of 40 yards. Draw an aiming point on this paper that is clearly visible to you when you get back to the firing line. Now, take a stepladder—that's right, a plain old stepladder—out of the garage or cellar and use it as a shooting rest. This will ensure that you have the aimed shot you require in test firing. Shooting a shotgun from a shooting bench—a table platform from which rifles are shot to ensure maximum bracing for extreme accuracy—will just about dismember your shoulder, so use the stepladder and stand up so that the recoil will not disturb you.

Bring along at least five each (ten is better) of all the different kinds of shells you feel are suitable for your kind of game and hunting. Using the ladder rest, carefully aim and fire. Identify the load used on each paper (a felt marking pen works well), and change the paper after each shot. When all the shells have been fired, scribe a 30-inch circle around the densest part of each pattern, count the enclosed holes and figure the percentage of your load which struck within the circle. Get an average of the five (or ten) shells of each load tested. You may be surprised at how much the individual—supposedly identical—shells vary! You may also be surprised to learn that your barrel, stamped "Modified," say, delivers improved cylinder or full choke patterns with some loads. One reason you do this testing is to find out such things. But perhaps the most important thing you'll learn is that, with one of the loads tried, your gun gives precisely the kind of patterns you need for your hunting. That's the load to shoot. It pays big dividends.

6 | FIELD TACTICS, GUN CARRIES AND THROWS

Throwing the twelfth strike in a perfect bowling game is almost anticlimactic; it must be remembered that it required eleven strikes to get to this position. The same applies to shooting a shotgun. While you have gained in proficiency, you may still be lacking in the experience and finesse that are part and parcel of becoming a polished shot. Strange as it may sound, you can spot a good gun handler by the way he assembles his piece, by the way he carries it, by the sure confidence he has when he takes his shotgun in hand. While gun handling is a habit, one that sets you aside from every other person you will hunt with from now on, good habits are learned actions. Like all learned actions, they require practice to acquire.

This is not a chapter on gun safety—that will appear later in the book. Rather, it is a chapter on gun handling; and while safety and handling should and do go hand in hand, both are equally important in the business of becoming a good rather than a mediocre shot.

Gun throws, those gorgeous blurs of motion that transform a carried shotgun into a lethally aimed instrument, are motions as intricate as the basic gun mount. They require hours of practice for flawless execution. They require visual practice (again in front of your mirror), and they have to be analyzed every bit as carefully as the fundamental mount. Basically, a gun throw is taking the shotgun from a comfortable carry position to the shooting position in one fluid, seemingly easy movement. No man can carry his shotgun all day long in the same position. Hands become weary and arms get tired. The field carries brought out in this chapter are the most comfortable ones I have managed to find in my years of hunting, based not only on my own personal tastes but also on those of others.

The basic field carry is the one from which you began your basic mount—that of a low port-arms position—with the shotgun held barrel up to the left and butt down to the right across your body. It is from this position, really a ready position, that you can mount your shotgun to your shoulder with the least amount of effort. But to attempt to carry your gun in this position all day long would be folly. The alternatives are fairly limited. We shall deal with five basic carries and the throws from them. One point here: all carries and mounts from carries are described for the *right-handed* shot. If you are left-handed, simply reverse the process.

You have already learned one carry and the throw from it in your basic gun mount, that of low port. All other throws stem from this basic mounting position, placing the shotgun in firing attitude the same way, all with a minimum of effort on your part. While throws do require a bit of manual dexterity, all are easy to learn with practice. Let's take them apart individually.

THE LEFT-ARM CRADLE

The shotgun is carried as you would a child, in the cradle of your left forearm and elbow (Plate 38). The fore end rests in the inside cup of your left elbow, with the left hand enclosing the trigger assembly and safety mechanism. The barrel rides above the horizontal about 30 degrees, keeping it well above a line of parallel to the ground. You should never use this carry when you have a companion on your left (or on your right if you are a left-handed shooter).

The throw from a left-hand cradle position should start with the left shoulder. The shoulder moves forward in a sharp motion (Plate 39), lifting the left elbow in a swinging movement. The elbow cup propels the fore end of your shotgun out and away from your body where it is met by the left hand, which swings away and out from your body. The right hand picks up the released trigger and safety assembly in midflight, completing the mounting motion as it does in the basic mount, pulling the stock up and into the shoulder pocket. The safety is released in this same motion, and the shotgun is in firing readiness when the butt meets the shoulder (Plate 40). Of all gun throws aside from the basic low port, this is the easiest to learn once you have mastered the basic mount.

THE RIGHT-SHOULDER CARRY

Perhaps the most restful position of all, this is also one of the safest. The shotgun is placed on the right shoulder, sighting plane down, trigger assembly and fore end up (Plate 41). The butt is carried low, and the muzzle rides up high out of harm's way. The right hand cups the trigger guard and safety mechanism, with the index and middle fingers riding relaxed and extended to shield them.

The throw from the shoulder starts, as all throws do, with the shoulder moving up and forward (Plate 42). Your body bends slightly at the waist,

Left-Arm Cradle

When using the left-arm cradle, the shotgun is carried comfortably by your left forearm and elbow (PLATE 38, ABOVE LEFT). The barrel rides well above the horizontal. The throw from a left-arm cradle starts with the left shoulder. In PLATE 39 (ABOVE RIGHT) you will see that the shoulder is well forward and that the cup of the left elbow has propelled the barrels up and out from the body to meet the extended left hand and arm. The right trigger finger has entered the trigger guard and the thumb is in the process of releasing the safety. The eyes are fixed on the rising target. In PLATE 40 (LEFT) the shotgun is in full shooting position, safety released, and eyes directly over the sighting plane of the barrels.

Perhaps the most restful of all carries, the right-shoulder carry (PLATE 41, RIGHT) is the one preferred by a majority of good gun handlers. In PLATE 42 (BELOW LEFT) the right shoulder has propelled the barrel up and over toward the target. The left hand and arm are going into full extension to meet the descending fore end. The trigger finger has entered the trigger guard, and the thumb, having already released the safety, is settling into full grip position around the tang. Note that the eyes are not watching the gun, but the target. In the process of completing the full mount (PLATE 43, BELOW RIGHT) the author's left hand has clasped the fore end while the right hand and arm are raising the stock into the shouldering position.

Right-Shoulder Carry

and the left hand rides up and out to meet the descending fore end in its cupped position. The right hand releases the safety and pulls the butt up and into position for firing. All of this is accomplished in one motion.

THE RIGHT-HAND CARRY

Though this carry (Plate 44) is preferred by many gunners, it is not one that I use until the day starts to come to an end and my arms and hands are becoming weary. The weight of the gun is absorbed entirely by the right hand and forearm, and it does tend to weigh you down after a while. The throw is no slower than any of the others, but it takes a little more precise timing to accomplish.

The throw from a right-hand carry starts with the right shoulder moving forward, swinging the right arm up and away from the body. Bear in mind that your hand has been holding the shotgun at its balance point, ahead of the action and just short of the fore end. To free this hand and get it back into position behind the trigger guard requires that you release your grip and allow the gun to slide ahead through your cupped relaxed fingers. As the trigger guard clears your fingers, you close your hand into firing position, releasing the safety at the same time (Plate 45).

Your left hand meanwhile has met the fore end out and away from your body, crossing out and over to effect this rendezvous (Plate 46). As the safety is cleared by the right hand, this hand also completes the moving of the stock up and rearward into firing attitude at the shoulder. *This throw requires a good deal of practice. Do not use it until you know it!*

THE RIGHT-HIP CARRY

In the years I hunted with my father, I found this to be one of his favorites. While not a position from which you can achieve gun speed to any great extent, it is a comfortable carry once you have mastered the throw from this position. What the hip carry does is to settle the weight of your shotgun where it does not bother you, directly over your hip. (See Plates 47 and 48.)

The shotgun is cradled in a cupped right hand, again at the balance point of the gun. Your hand is slightly open to protect the trigger and safety assembly from brush and trash. The palm of your hand holds the shotgun against your hip just above your belt line so that the gun hangs in place. The barrel is held slightly down, and the stock floats a bit high to the rear.

The mount starts the same here as the right-hand carry, with a swinging forward of the right arm and shoulder. The cupped right hand slides down over the trigger assembly into firing position, releasing the safety as it arrives

Right-Hand Carry

Perhaps the most difficult of all gun throws, and one that should never be used in the field without extensive practice, the right-hand carry (PLATE 44, ABOVE LEFT) is used at day's end or while traversing heavy brush. In the middle of the right-hand throw, the author's hand has come from the balance point ahead of the trigger guard, cupping itself to allow the trigger guard to slip through the now released fingers, to grasp the pistol grip firmly with the last three fingers of the right hand. The thumb is in the process of pushing off the safety while the right trigger finger is just about to enter the trigger guard. The left hand and arm are starting their upward and forward swing to meet the descending fore end (PLATE 45, ABOVE CENTER). In PLATE 46 (ABOVE RIGHT) the right hand is lifting the stock into shoulder position while the left hand and arm continue to straighten to complete the mount.

Right-Hip Carry

Another restful position is the right-hip carry (PLATE 47, ABOVE LEFT). The right hand grips the gun at the balance point ahead of the trigger guard while the right thumb finds purchase at the top of your belt to form a brace. Again, do not use this throw until you have practiced it extensively. In PLATE 48 (ABOVE RIGHT), the right hand is in position around the pistol grip, having allowed the trigger guard to slide through opened, released fingers from the balance point. The trigger finger has entered the trigger guard while the thumb is releasing the safety. The left hand and arm are at full extension to meet the descending barrels and fore end. The right hand has the stock and butt nearly to solid shooting position.

at full grip. The left arm comes out and across your body, with the left hand cupped to meet the fore end as it arrives in extended reach. The right hand pulls the stock up and rearward into firing attitude. *Once again, practice this throw before using it in the field!*

A great deal of stress is placed on balance in shooting. Even more is said of foot position. As I remarked earlier, it is my feeling that when a field shot begins to think about his feet, that is the day his shooting will go downhill. Foot position, aside from basic common sense that it is preferable to have your feet somewhere near normal balance position, actually is not so important as you might assume. What is important is balance. How you arrive at this is something else entirely.

A good prize fighter is never off balance. Neither is a good wing shot. Regardless of the cover or terrain he is traversing, a good wing shot is always in an attitude of carriage from which he can recover rapidly. Much of this balance and carriage is predetermined; he should never commit himself to a movement from which he cannot recover instantly. All of this has to come from your style of walking.

It is not my intention to teach you how to walk all over again. Rather, what I want you to do is to learn to walk on uneven ground cover. The style is entirely different from the stride you use daily. In your normal stride the weight of your body descends through your leg to an impact point at the heel. A field stride rolls the weight forward through the ball of your foot to the toes. In a field step, all weight is consciously held forward, so that you are imitating the old step of the Indian scouts.

A field stride is shorter than a normal stride for two basic reasons. First, rough ground makes it difficult for you to take a step of normal size. Second, long steps are balance-losers: they put you in a position where an instant recovery requires the grace of a ballet dancer. As a result, we must shorten our stride to hold ourselves in readiness. One cardinal rule of field balance is that a right-handed shot *always* steps over an object on the ground with his *left foot first*. This gives you that split-second advantage over a flushing bird taking off while you are in the middle of your stride.

We all cross fences while hunting. Here is a tip that will get you at least one bird over the next three hunting seasons. As you approach a fence, do so slowly, with an uneven pace. Stop short of it and pause for a moment before going right up to the fence. If a bird is lying there, he will flush when you stop. If he lies through this move (and some do), *and you are hunting alone*, go through the fence with your left leg and gun barrel at the same time. Follow through with your body and right leg. This puts you back into shooting position far faster than any other method I know. If you are hunting with a partner, one of you should be on the lookout as the other goes through the fence, to take care of any late-flushing game.

Have you ever noticed that you have a tendency to become careless in the field and begin looking at a particular object rather than at the whole landscape within your field of vision? Your eyes should be wide open, roughly focused about 100 feet ahead of you. This allows peripheral vision to take care of any activity that might occur to either side of you. I try consciously not to look at any one thing in particular; instead I attempt to take in the whole area with my sweep of vision. In doing so, I gain a head start on a flushing bird, a start that gives me the slight advantage I may need to bring him down.

If a bird flushes on the blind side of a tree or a clump of brush away from you, take two or three running strides to either side. This maneuver will give

PLATE 49. When you stop for a smoke during the course of a day's hunting, always deactivate the firing capability of your shotgun. In this drawing both gunners are using doubles. The man on the left has opened the action and keeps his thumb over both chambers. The man on the right has opened and unloaded his double and leaned it against a nearby log. Both are sound safety practices.

you an open shot more times than not. While you should always approach a blind clump or tree directly to take care of a bird flushing out of either side, you can get clear in the space of an instant if you take those all-important steps. I learned that many years ago when grouse were plentiful and good grouse dogs were scarce. This trick applies to all of our upland game birds as well.

Hunting without a dog makes it mandatory that you mark your own downed game carefully where it falls. Marking means never taking your eyes from the spot where the bird touched the ground. But two operations *must* be performed, in this instance, without looking at them. First, *you put your gun on safe!* Second, *you reload your gun!* I have had supposedly dead birds rise to fly again as I approached them. Had I not reloaded as I was approaching, I would be standing there with an empty gun and a silly look on my face. Remember these two points: Place the shotgun back on safe, and reload. Doing so, you are ready for any eventuality.

Several years ago a close friend of mine, a man whom I hunt with fairly regularly, had a horrifying experience. He had been plagued by a sticky safety—actually had trouble getting his safety free so that the gun would fire. To overcome this nuisance (and as long as he was hunting alone), he manhandled the gun off-safe and carried it the rest of the day ready to fire. His big setter came down on a tight point late in the day, and my friend walked in to flush the bird. At that moment he made a mistake that he will have to live with the rest of his days. He stumbled, and the right barrel cut his favorite dog almost in half. He finished him with the left barrel and went home heartbroken.

The movement of releasing a safety is so much a part of the gun-mounting process that it should never, ever, have to be a conscious motion. The gun is ready to fire when it reaches your shoulder. As a result, there is no excuse for your ever having the safety released *until* you are ready to fire. Hunting with any firearm off-safe is asking for trouble—a foolhardy stunt at best.

None of us likes to hunt right straight through a day without pausing for a smoke or a talk with our companions to plan strategy. Here is another pointer that will prevent accidents when you stop to sit down. If you are carrying a double gun, open it. If you are shooting a pump (repeater), simply release the action and let it slide back about a half inch before you sit down. With a semiautomatic shotgun, your best bet is to unload completely.

Never lay any gun on the ground in an operative condition—safety on or not. I saw a romping young dog step on the safety of a pump, shove it through with his paw, and discharge the gun—all in one movement. It scared the living hell out of the party, but there were no casualties. Always deactivate your firearm before it leaves your hands, and accidents like this can never happen.

7 | SIMPLIFIED SKEET SHOOTING

The great rise in popularity of skeet shooting may be attributed mainly to the fact that it is so much fun. Admittedly, the game of skeet is a substitute for actual hunting for fur and feathers. As a training method for field shooting, skeet is a shade light in the balance, and has to be used judiciously. Because it is so enjoyable in itself, however, and because it provides a means of keeping one's shooting form in trim during the off seasons, skeet cannot be overlooked in any conscientious approach to shotguns and shooting.

The name of the game, *skeet,* comes from a Scandinavian word meaning "shoot." While it was invented before 1925, it was not until that time, when the National Skeet Shooting Association was formed, that the sport gained any degree of popularity. Today, skeet (with its blood brother trap) accounts for a large percentage of the shotgun shells fired each year in the United States, a fact that makes ammunition company executives beam with joy.

Skeet is a game of fixed angles and target speeds. The bird (or target) flies in the same direction from the same place at the same rate of speed each time, under normal conditions. (Wind, the constant bugaboo of many sports, does have a tendency to affect radically the scores of the shoot-by-the-numbers hand on a skeet field.) It is for these reasons that not all good skeet shooters are good field shots. Dealing as they do with repetition shooting, they may be successful at skeet without being capable of the instantaneous adjustment necessary in field shooting, where no two shots are ever the same.

The model for this chapter on skeet is a good friend of mine, Gene Smith, who ranks as one of the very few fine shots of my acquaintance. He has that gorgeous sense of timing—and few people do—that makes shotgun shooting seem simple. I used him as my model for the simple reason that he embodies every aspect of the relaxed shooting method I have chosen to call Contraflex. He sweeps, but will deny it to his dying day. He is extremely argumentative, but always refreshingly so, and a gentleman. He is of a rare breed.

Skeet more or less deals with an "over the shoulder" look at the sport of shotgun shooting in that nearly half the targets presented to you come from your off-gun shoulder. It is far easier for a right-handed shot to take a right-to-left-crossing bird than it is for him to deal with the reverse, since he seems to track better with his left shoulder than with his right. I know that it took me far longer to deal satisfactorily with a right-shoulder track than it did with one where my left side led the way. The same applied in skiing: I could turn like a champion to the left, but sliding my skiis to the right was a learned motion.

Skeet shooting, properly done, is rapid shooting. A polished skeet shot may mess around on station for several seconds getting his foot and body position just so, but when he calls for his target he breaks it—immediately. Rarely does he let it get by the midfield center stake. This growth of swing, this learned motion, requires hours of practice to build into your system of shotgun shooting. It is an advantage only in skeet and detracts from, rather than adds to one's skill in field shooting.

Remember when we spoke of the three determinants we must possess to adjust a shot to strike a moving target? We said then that we had to know the deflection, speed, and range of our target to arrange for a charge of shot to meet it at a predetermined spot in the air. We know all this in skeet. The target deflections are built in, and never vary. With built-in deflections and built-in stations from which to shoot our birds, range is naturally standardized. Target speed is controlled by the throwing device, or trap, and never varies more than a few feet per second from one day to the next—certainly never enough to require any major readjustment in timing. How, then, you may well ask, do trained skeet shots miss birds? For two reasons: either they get careless or they lose their sense of concentration.

The shooting stations of a skeet field are laid out on an arc of a circle, with seven stands, or shooting stations, arranged around the perimeter of this arc, and an eighth station planted directly in the center of the field between the two trap houses. To the left, as we look toward midfield from Station 4, is the High House; to the right is the Low House. The longest leads on a skeet field are found at No. 3 Low House and No. 5 High House.

When I went through Primary Gunnery Training in the Navy, we were taught skeet shooting as a method of determining the all-important angle of deflection required in air-to-air fire. We shot with weapons equipped with ring sights. We were taught to lead a bird by so many target radii, or "rads." Once a student learned that the lead at a given station was a rad and a half, all he had to do was establish this lead, keep his barrel moving at the speed needed to continue this deflection, and pull the trigger. What he did not

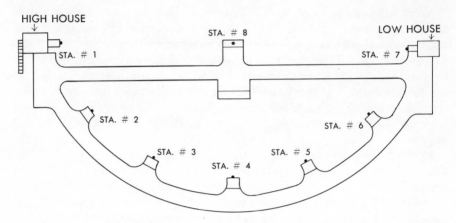

PLATE 50.   Skeet field layout.

learn was to make these adjustments automatically, without reference to sighting aids. It did make a fair aerial gunner out of him, but never a good one. The good ones were the boys who adjusted without thinking, and there were precious few of them around at the time. Pilots used to fight over the good ones.

Like any sport requiring a learned set of motions, skeet has been surrounded with an aura of mystique, a degree of difficulty that is actually not present. A good field shot can become an excellent skeet shot with a small amount of practice. In reverse, it may take a good skeet shot a long time to get to be a superior field shot. Here is where the twin aids of Contraflex and sweep shooting take over.

The first time that you walk out on a skeet field, you will learn that there are all manner of shotgun shots. You have the Croucher, the man who addresses each station as if he were coiled to strike. You have the Foot-Position Addict, the man who methodically cleans off his station as if he were the local janitor and then takes a good half minute to get his left and right foot in *exactly* the right position. You have the Gun Adjuster, who has to mount and remount his shotgun *ad nauseam,* until it feels absolutely perfect. And last, you have the Dry Tracker, the man who swings through the projected arc of his target not once but several times, to satisfy himself that it hasn't changed from the last time he shot it a half hour ago. (It hasn't.)

A man I know who flies as chief pilot for one of our major airlines is also one of the finest shots I have ever had the pleasure of watching in action. Whatever he does he does beautifully, and with such ridiculous lack of effort that it fairly makes you weep for the sheer beauty of it. A shotgun is a wand in his hands, one that he wields with consummate ease. He was the man who first put the idea of sweep shooting in my head—but not by what he said, for he still deals in feet and inches today. By the simple expedient of watching him in action I suddenly fell over the obvious that I had been overlooking for years. Yet Kaye, for all the beauty of his motions, missed birds from time to time.

I spoke of lack of concentration as being one of the major reasons that good skeet shots miss birds. This is a very important fact. Competitive skeet shooting requires the same amount of dedication from its devotees that tournament golf does from the touring professionals. Good skeet shots are not casual shots. They may give the impression of being casual, but this is nothing more than an effort on their part to remain relaxed while shooting. They have to dedicate themselves to each bird, for even the easiest shot can be missed by a person who lets his mind wander.

Kaye and Gene Smith are two of the most relaxed shots I have ever seen. They step up on station with a light, springy stride, settle themselves without paying attention to where their feet or their hands are (they know), and call

PLATE 51. Gene Smith is one of the most relaxed skeet shots I have ever met. Here on Station No. 1 you will notice that he takes a very narrow stance, raising his gun barrel a full 45 degrees above the horizontal so that he is in position to take the bird, which will come from above and directly behind him. The stock butt is in perfect position, while the left hand and forearm are at near full extension. Waiting members of his squad stand quietly away from the station so as not to distract him when he calls for his target.

for the target. The bird is broken with effortless ease, with a minimum of "grandstanding" for the gallery. They are sufficiently relaxed to make it look like a lead-pipe cinch, for they know, when they make it seem easy, that they are doing the job well.

With these two men as our examples, it is obvious that scoring at skeet requires no less than great effort to remain relaxed while you are swinging through and sweeping your bird from the sky with one clean, fluid motion. If you remember to *sweep,* and remember to *lead with your off-target shoulder,* you will hit your birds consistently. When you miss them—and you will— you will find that you either stopped sweeping (and without this action your barrel stops) or that your swing was jerky and uneven (caused by yanking the gun through without leading your swing with your off shoulder).

Save me from the Foot-Position Addict who favors this stance on one station and that stance on another. His is an extremely artificial approach to shooting. To my mind, the most important function of a skeet field is to give sportsmen the minimum amount of practice that they need to keep their shooting form polished up. When the field shot starts converting ("subverting" would be more appropriate) the shooting form he has learned afield to the mechanical approach that some trained competitive skeet shots use to score in tournaments, he immediately begins losing the ground he has gained in actual hunting.

Scoring at skeet requires getting the edge on the target. Taking the ability to shoot well as a norm, the man who puts himself in a position of advantage by getting the edge is the man who hits one or two more birds a round. The advantage may be slight, measured in terms of a second or two, but the fact that you have it going for you (as does every good skeet hand I know) is the difference.

People who miss targets are people who let targets get the best of them. They continue to worry about the bird they lost instead of taking each bird as it comes. If they miss one, they are likely to miss another, or even two or three more targets while worrying about the one they dropped originally. Like a bad shot in golf, the miss is past history; forget it if you hope to climb into the upper scoring brackets.

The only way to get a jump on a target on a skeet field is to do it station by station. There are simple little adjustments that you can learn to make automatically so that you have no conscious feeling of settling yourself into a pattern. But before dealing with these adjustments, let's talk about one important factor that too many of us overlook.

In American-style skeet, you do not mount your gun, as you do in the field, when the bird appears; rather, you have it shouldered and cheeked *before* you call for the target. I have seen men shoot skeet by leaving their guns in a field carry while they call for their targets, and some gunners turn in impressive scores this way; in fact, International-style skeet rules require starting with the gun down. However, for our purpose here, which is mainly to stress the importance—the absolute necessity—of sweeping through your targets if you are to hit consistently, it is simpler to begin with the gun mounted. With the gun down, the average beginner at skeet would hurry his mount to be certain of catching up with the bird while it was in range. This might take his mind off sweeping. I feel it is better at this stage of proficiency to take advantage of the rule which permits calling for the bird with the gun up.

Now, taking our skeet field station by station, let's learn the split-second edges.

STATION NO. 1

The High and the Low House birds from every station fly directly over the center stake set in the outfield by Station No. 8. Knowing this, you know your deflection. On No. 1 High House, mount your gun and raise the barrel to a 45-degree angle directly over the center stake. Raise your head slightly off the comb of the stock for improved vision and call for your target. It will appear directly over your muzzle. Now, hold a trifle *under* it and slap the trigger. More High House No. 1 targets are shot *over* than are ever shot under.

On the incoming Low House No. 1 bird, let it fly to you and then sweep it out of the sky. Do not hurry this shot; rather, make it a mechanical sure thing.

STATION NO. 2

Of all the birds on a skeet field, this is the one that seems to give everyone the most trouble. Coming, as it does, from your off shoulder, the target has a tendency to get the jump on inexperienced shooters. It should not. Stand comfortably in the station, check your shotgun, and point it out over the center stake *even with the top* of the High House. Now, swing back toward the High House and lay your barrel about 8 feet ahead of the trap chute. As you call for your bird, start a perceptible swing along the line of flight. Your bird will catch up to your barrel as you break it easily.

Here, again, the Low House bird is an incomer and is taken as it nears you and slows. Sweep it down.

PLATE 52. Standing comfortably on Station No. 3, Gene Smith points his gun barrel approximately 6 feet ahead of the High House chute exit to get a slight advantage on the emerging target.

STATION NO. 3

The High House bird is still a quartering outgoer, and fairly easy. *Don't forget to point that barrel at a spot about 6 feet from the trap-house chute* when you call for your target. Again, start your swing as you call.

The Low House bird here is the one requiring more lead than any other Low House target on the field. Here it is mandatory that you sweep with a pronounced follow-through or you will lose it at once.

STATION NO. 4

For some reason, this pair of birds gives every new shooter difficulty. A full 90-degree deflection shot, No. 4 Station is not nearly so demanding as No. 3, but many shooters make it so. Starting at the center stake, swing back to the trap-house chute (3 to 4 feet ahead of it is perfect) and call for your target as you anticipate your swing. You do the same on both birds. Remember to sweep through and past, and you should never miss them.

STATION NO. 5

This is the transition station. It is here that your High House birds become incomers and your Low House targets become outgoers. However, the same rules apply as they did on the other side of the field. Taking the High House bird first, ride it in, sweep past and through, and break it. Bear in mind that the High House No. 5 bird is again a major lead on the field. Swing back to a spot 6 feet ahead of the Low House trap chute and call for the target, starting your swing a touch ahead of visual sighting of the target. Sweep through it and break it.

STATION NO. 6

The incoming High House bird is a piece of cake shot here *if* you let it come to you and then sweep it. The outgoing Low House bird should be anticipated, swept through, and broken near or just past the center stake in the outfield. If you let this bird fly too far, you give it the advantage of sliding through a dispersed pattern.

PLATE 53. In the middle of full sweep, Gene picks up the target, accelerates through it, and blasts it into bits with his sweep. Again, notice his completely relaxed shooting position.

STATION NO. 7

You should *never* miss either one of these targets under any circumstances. Let the incoming High House bird fly to you, and sweep it into dust. The outgoing Low House bird will fly 8 feet over the center stake. Place your barrel there and take the target as you see it.

STATION NO. 8

This is the station that literally terrifies a new shooter. It is a violently short incomer, flying over the center stake above and out from you. Like a sand shot in golf, once learned, it is simple.

PLATE 54. In shooting position on No. 8 station, Gene Smith places his gun barrel on the lower-right-hand corner of the High House trap chute. Note that his toes are pointed directly toward the outfield and that his body is pivoted back into shooting position.

On the High House target, stand on station with your toes pointing at the center stake. Shoulder and cheek your shotgun and point it high over the stake, at about a 70-degree angle. Now come back to the High House trap chute and lay your muzzle on the *lower right-hand corner*. Start your swing as you call for the bird, and sweep it right out of the sky. Remember to lead your swing with your right shoulder, and sweep, and you'll break it regularly.

The Low House bird flies to your left and over the center stake. Angle your toes at a 20-degree angle toward your left. Mount your gun at a 50-degree angle and then come back to the trap chute and lay your muzzle on the *lower left-hand corner* of the door. Call for your bird as you start your swing, and sweep it out of the sky.

Both of these shots are rapid, seemingly with no lag between bird sighting and shot. Keep it that way and you will score well here.

PLATE 55. Taking the bird in a full sweep, Gene breaks it directly over the center stake.

PLATE 56. If a malfunction of your shotgun occurs during a round of skeet, remain on station and call the referee. Notice that the members of Gene's squad stay well clear while Gene and the referee attempt to clear the jam. Gene's shotgun barrel is pointed into the ground and toward the outfield, the proper position.

SHOOTING THE DOUBLES

Eight of your 25 birds on a skeet field are thrown in pairs, coming from the High and Low houses simultaneously. The rules of the game call for you to shoot at the bird coming from *behind* you first. On stations No. 1 and No. 2, always break the High House bird first. On stations No. 6 and No. 7, always break the Low House bird first.

You do not have to hurry in shooting doubles. Just make sure that you break the first bird, and your troubles in this particular bit are over. Concentrate on one bird at a time. Swing through your first bird, break it, and then *leave it!* Reversing your swing, drop back to the incomer, sweep through it, and smash it. Do not try to rush your first bird. You will find that you can swing back and find the second target in plenty of time. After you have shot doubles a few times, you will set up a rhythm that makes these pairs become far easier than they appear to be at first glance.

There is a code of conduct that all good skeet shots follow. If you can learn the basics of this code, the chances of your acceptance in a good squad will be excellent:

1. Don't be a Helpful Harry. The guy who just missed a bird ahead of you couldn't care less why you think he missed it. Never volunteer information unless he turns to you and asks for it. Then, if you know, tell him. Otherwise, say nothing.

2. A skeet field is not a coffee klatch, so knock off the casual conversation. To break birds consistently, you have to concentrate. It is difficult to do so when two clowns are gabbing behind you.

3. *Never,* under any circumstances, load your shotgun before you step on station. The muzzle should be high and facing over the outfield when you load. While shooting singles, load *one* shell at a time. The only time you should load a pair is when you are working on doubles.

4. The scorekeeper's word is law: remember that. If he calls *"Lost,"* that bird is missed, regardless of what you think. Don't bicker with the man or argue in behalf of another gun. Just accept his ruling and move along.

5. In the event of any malfunction of your shotgun during a round, call the referee (scorekeeper) to the station. Point the muzzle toward the outfield and keep it there. Make any repairs on the spot as needed, but if you have a live round in the piece, *stay on station* until it is cleared.

6. All skeet guns should be unloaded while you are off station, but even so, no one likes to look down your muzzle. Keep that barrel either up or down at all times when you are not shooting.

7. When you are next to shoot, move into a position about 6 feet behind the shooter on station at the time. Stand there quietly until your turn comes, and then don't drag! Get up there, load, call for your birds, and get off!

8. When you call for your birds, do so audibly. Do not develop the habit of gargling or snarling for your bird. Simply say "Pull" for the High House bird, and "Mark it" for the Low House targets. Say it out loud so that the man who releases the trap can hear you plainly. This habit will, without delay, give you targets that fly when you expect them to fly.

One last word of advice: Never take this game (or yourself) so seriously that you overlook the basic premise behind it all. This is a sharpener, a method of practice. The moment you overdo it, your field shooting will suffer. Keep that in mind, and enjoy yourself.

8 | TRAPSHOOTING

The day they took away live pigeon shooting from many parts of the United States was a sad one indeed for American Saturday gunners in Granddad's heyday. Backed to the hilt by the Society for the Prevention of Cruelty to Animals, the pigeon ban drastically curtailed a sport that had endured for years. Each weekend it was possible to wager the farm, the corn crop for the next year or two, or every cow in the barn on the outcome of a head-to-head live bird match with your neighbor. If ego was the determinant, the sky was the limit.

The sport of trapshooting is far from a new one . . . nor was it new when the Great Pigeon Ban came into effect. Its historical roots go back to England, where we find it mentioned around the year 1720. Exactly when it arrived in America is anyone's guess. It was not until the formation of the American (or Amateur) Trapshooting Association and the arrival of the pigeon blight that anyone paid it much more than lip service. But Grandpa had to shoot at something, and if it couldn't be flesh and feathers it might just as well be clay targets.

An eggshell is a robust object when placed alongside a clay target. Weighing (as it must by rule) 3.5 ounces, give or take 5 percent, a clay target is 1⅛ inches in height and 4⁵⁄₁₆ inches in diameter. The boxes they are shipped in are marked "fragile as eggs," and the shippers mean it. Regardless of what the skeet and trap shooters of this nation think of each other, they both shoot the same target each weekend.

The name of the game came from the trap from which live birds were released. Today's traps are electrical in control, spring-activated, and set to throw the target not less than 48 nor more than 52 yards before it hits the ground. While the target's speed of emergence from the trap house is rapid, air resistance and its light weight slow it, causing it to fall sharply

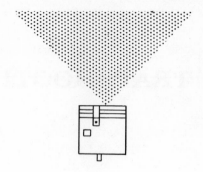

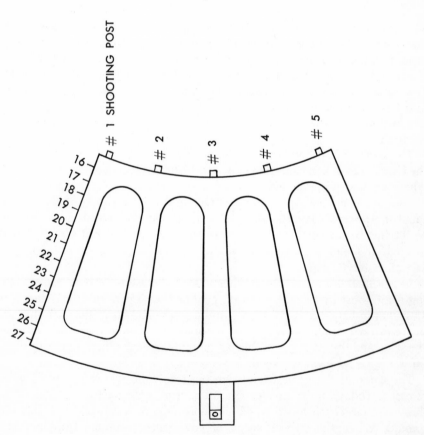

PLATE 57. Twenty-seven-yard trap field layout.

at the end of its flight path. Far more trap birds are missed because the charge of shot passes *over* them than are missed for any other reason. The instant a target crests—and it does so within a short distance—it begins to fall. The lead, if we were approaching this matter from the standpoint of lead rather than that of sweep shooting, would actually be under and ahead rather than over and ahead.

A trap field is laid out in five positions, all facing (in a shallow arc) a trap house set directly ahead of the firing line. From the front line of shooting positions, the trap house is set ahead 16 yards, the minimum distance allowed in the sport. From there, in accordance with ability, a shooter can be handicapped back to 27 yards, a truly horrible distance at which to shoot. Even under the kindest of circumstances, 27-yard shooters rarely catch up with their birds this side of 45 yards, and even a solid gun handler is in deep trouble when he first steps back to the rear of the field.

Trap is shot with the 5-man squad alternating on each of the 5 stations,

PLATE 58. Trap is shot with a five-man squad alternating on each of the five trap field stations. In this photo the shooter on No. 2 Station is in the process of calling for his target. The shooters on Nos. 1, 4 and 5 stations are quietly awaiting their turns. The shooter on No. 3 Station (the next man up) has his gun loaded with the action open so that he can close it and call for his bird without disrupting the pace of the squad.

25 shots making up a round. The birds are thrown from the trap house anywhere within 47 degrees on each side of the center line of the field, and thus do not afford the gunner the automatic deflection he finds on a skeet field. He does know target size and he does know target speed. Practice will give him target range, but the unknown-angle aspect of this sport does make it

PLATE 59.   Gene Hill, one of the best trap shots on the East Coast, shows here the exaggerated shooting position required for competitive trap. In this close-up you can see the high flare of his right elbow giving him a much more solid butt pocket to absorb recoil over a 200-bird match. His left hand cups the fore end comfortably with the left index finger riding along the center of the fore end to cup the very tip.

more difficult than skeet. Many skeet shooters will not admit this, but then I have never seen very many good trap shots come off skeet fields.

Range and unknown deflection make trap a difficult game. For best handling the long shots, tight chokes are chosen, and to make it easy to maintain a smooth swing, barrels are longer than on skeet guns. Long barrels probably make for more accurate pointing than short ones, too, a plus here where shooting is more deliberate than at skeet. Since the trap-shooter wants to keep the bird in view above his gun muzzle and still break it, trap gun stocks have high combs, and because trap loads are usually more powerful than those for skeet, the guns are made heavier to soak up recoil. The net effect of all this is that the trap gun is far longer and weighs considerably more than the skeet or field gun. It's a specialized tool for a highly competitive game. Whereas the skeet gun can be used for most upland hunting, the trap gun is out of place in the field except possibly for long-range waterfowl shooting or turkey hunting.

Over-unders are popular with trapshooters for various reasons, one prac-tical one being that the two tubes give two chokes; thus the same gun can be used for 16-yard matches with the modified barrel and for long-range handicap shooting with the full choke.

A trap stance is a mechanical stance, unlike the one you have learned thus far. Compared with the field shooting position we have taught, the trap stance is squarer by far to the line of fire, with the right elbow flared high and out from the shoulder. The shooting is precise and studied. All in all, trap, like skeet, is fine as a practice tool; but the game has a tendency to turn a good field shot into a mediocre one in short order if he overdoes it.

Earlier in this book, I mentioned Rudy Etchen, to my mind one of the finest trapshooters I have ever had the pleasure of watching in action. John Sternberger is another, a polished mechanical practitioner of the sport whose moves stand out when he shoots in competition. John makes trapshooting look easy, when in actuality it is not. He does so for the basic reason that he is so practiced in every facet of it that there is seemingly no conscious effort on his part to put shot and target together. John, unwittingly, put me on the track of the teaching method I use today on trap, one I call the Go System.

Far too many shooters—and this is especially true of beginners—are ex-tremists. They are either too fast or too slow. In trapshooting, to be too slow is to handicap yourself unnecessarily. Once you start thinking of the position of your barrel in relation to the target, you require an additional split second to combine two factors, and that time, together with a bird that is rarely broken within 30 yards of your shooting position, portends disaster.

Good trapshooters have timing that is a joy to watch. They all seem to break their birds at the same instant . . . just as the target nears full cresting in its flight arc. Rarely will you see a long-yardage handicap shooter let a bird get ahead of him. Only when his concentration is broken or when he gets careless does he spot the target the 3 to 5 yards that could spell a miss. Rather, he takes the bird with a precise flick of his barrel, breaking it with a

PLATE 60.   In full trap shooting stance, Gene Hill shows a pronounced forward lean with the entire body, the weight well forward on the left side. Again, notice the pronounced flare of the right shooting elbow.

rapid movement of hand, body, and eye that can come only from hours of practice.

The Go System is a method of timing that allows you to take your target faster, and therefore with a better chance of accuracy. Combining an additional factor with Contraflex (see Chapter 3) and sweep shooting (see Chapter 4), the Go System makes you take the bird as you see it, apparently without time for thought on your part. It will work equally well in open-field shooting for plains pheasant or in a goose or duck blind on a cold winter morning. It does give you an edge—and that is an advantage in any sport.

In trapshooting, approach stance as you would in a comfortable field-shooting position. The additional barrel length of the gun will require you to make a small adjustment, but aside from this, change nothing else in your approach to mounting and cheeking your shotgun. You may be told many times that if you change so and so, you will be a far better trap shot. You might, but your ability to down game will suffer.

There are all kinds of theories attached to this sport, especially regarding the moot question of where you should place your gun barrel before calling for your bird. It really doesn't make much difference as long as you have your gun muzzle pointed somewhere out over the trap house. The bird is going to come as a surprise to you in any case, so why worry about trying to second-guess the angle? Take your stance comfortably, settle the shotgun solidly into a hold about a foot over the trap house roof, and call for your bird. This applies to all five shooting positions of a trap field.

We have learned that sweep shooting allows you to overlook lead entirely. The sweep is a deadly advantage on a trap field. Instead of a prolonged follow-through such as you used in skeet, trap sweeping is almost a flick of the barrel through the line of flight of the target. The slap of the trigger combines with this flick to give you a shot that puts the bird down well inside the 35-yard mark.

Look at the trap field as a whole over the sighting plane of your shotgun. Keep both eyes wide open and do not focus on anything in particular, even the muzzle of your gun. What you are interested in lies out there within a 94-degree spread some 30-odd yards away. You know where your muzzle is; it follows your eyes—so forget it. What you want is the first sight of that target so that you can pick up its deflection angle immediately.

Once the target shows in the outfield sky, swing the barrel *up and through* the flight path with a pronounced flick of the left hand on the fore end of your shotgun. The right hand is seating the butt plate solidly at your shoulder, thus making your left hand the pointing instrument. *Use it!* The instant your muzzle flicks through the flight path of the target, slap the trigger and let the shot go. It may sound as if you are hurrying the shot. Rather, it is the opposite. All you are doing is taking the shot when it is ready to be taken instead of waiting for a double check to be sure. You will miss far fewer birds this way than you will by double-checking.

There is only one exception to the Go rule—the straightaway target. All you do on a straightaway is shoot directly at it! Cover it with your muzzle, and touch off the shot. Covering it ensures that you break it as it *rises* into the pattern instead of shooting under it. On all other deflections of targets, flick away to your heart's content.

There are three variations of trapshooting that should be dealt with here, ones that have gained immensely in popularity over the past few years. Let's take them individually.

INTERNATIONAL TRAP

International Trap involves the shooting of a single target at a time, with the target flying at a far greater speed at any demented angle the trap happens to throw it. You can get "grasscutters" slanting off and falling fast, or you can get a high, towering target that seems bent on getting into orbit before you catch up with it. Shot from 17 yards, International Trap is more fun than any other shotgun game I have ever seen. To say that it is different is an understatement.

You are allowed two shots at each target in International Trap. After you shoot one round you will see why. I should guess that easily 40 percent of your targets broken in a round of this insanity are caught by the second shell in your gun. Never take the chance of being so sure of a target that you do not fire a second time at it. Use a pair of shells on every target, and your scoring will show the difference.

If ever a game was invented for the field shot, International Trap would have to be it. Here, an experienced field hand has an advantage over a shooter who is set in his ways. Accustomed as he is to birds that fly wherever they feel like going, he is not taken aback by the International target. He is far more likely to accept its behavior as standard. But if there ever was a spot for your sweep-shooting experience to pay off, it is here.

Don't be shy about getting off that first shot in a hurry in this game. The instant your left hand flicks through the escaping target, bust off a shot, and *keep that barrel moving!* Now get off a second shot just to be dead certain you have a broken target. Carroll Kinsey, motel owner from Thurmont, Maryland, is the man responsible for introducing me to this sport. Carroll is a superb shot in the field. When I say that he does not take the time to fool around on a thrown bird, I would be unfair to his ability. He strikes at them with the speed of a snake, breaking them the instant he has access. Whether

Carroll is a sweep shot by habit is anyone's guess, but sweep he does—and in deadly fashion.

SHOOTING TRAP DOUBLES

Francis Cole, goose-shooting expert from Oxford, Maryland, talked me into entering my first doubles tournament, even before I had even shot at a pair on a trap field. Ten minutes' coaching on the clubhouse porch sent me on my way. I broke an amazing (as I was told later) 87 by 100 targets, and walked away fairly satisfied, but still unhappy about several I *knew* I should have had with ease.

In Trap Doubles, you are dealing with two types of targets. Except on Station 3, one will always fly straight away from you, the other going off at a deflection angle. *Always break the straightaway target first!* This is the easy one, the piece of cake of the pair. Deal with the deflection bird after you handle the straightaway.

Trap Doubles are shot at 16 yards, and here your shotgun should be an over-under. The reasoning behind this is threefold—speed, choke selectivity and the single sighting plane. The first target is taken just as quickly as you can get on it, and this requires a gun you can point rapidly. A fast shooter will take this bird at about 30 yards, so even an improved cylinder choke will do the job. Never is anything tighter than a modified bore needed here.

The second bird is slowing down and falling a shade by the time you catch up with it. It's usually taken inside the 45-yard mark, some experts breaking it at about 40. For these, barrels choked improved cylinder and modified will serve, their wide patterns complementing the fast shooting. Gunners who are a trifle more deliberate in shooting will prefer a modi-fied/full combination, to break birds a few yards farther out.

Sweep shooting pays big dividends in Trap Doubles. Without this training, I doubt if I would have scored anywhere near as well as I did the first time I shot it. Instead of shooting mechanically, or worrying about both birds simultaneously, I was taking each bird as a separate entity in itself, an ap-proach that still pays off today. Never concern yourself with more than one target at a time. Forget about the second bird until you have given the first your best effort. You will find the second still within excellent shooting range when you arrive on it.

LONG-YARDAGE TRAPSHOOTING

Of all the shooting done at clay targets, none is more difficult than long-yardage trap. Here your target looks like a bumblebee as it takes off from the trap house, and the field stretching out in all its glory before you looks a full mile long. People have been known to get the palsy the first time they shoot the 27-yard distance, and I can readily see why.

By the time you catch up with a bird from the back line, it is a good 45 yards away. Even if presented to you flat, a claybird would be a circle only $4\frac{5}{16}$ inches in diameter—and it's never seen in that attitude. The normal target is something about midway between an edge view, which is a rectangle $1\frac{1}{8}$ x $4\frac{5}{16}$ inches in size with the top two corners knocked off, and a full circle. If you are to hit such a tiny target consistently almost half a football field away, even with a perfect hold, your pattern must be dense. Twenty-seven-yard shooters almost invariably choose the choke and load which will give them the tightest possible pattern.

If the gunner fires from 27 yards with about the same timing as he does from 16, the relationship he sees between the gun muzzle and the target will be similar at both distances. However, if he slows down, as many do, in order to perfect his hold, the bird will get far enough away that it will be dropping fairly rapidly due to its velocity loss at long range, while at the same time continuing to move away. This greatly complicates the shooter's job. It's best to get your shots off before this target drop becomes pronounced. If this is difficult to do, you'll have to learn to hold lower, which can be a problem with the typical high-shooting trap gun. Some shooters use adjustable butt plates which permit them to raise the stock higher while maintaining good shoulder contact, thus tipping the muzzle lower and building in an automatic lead for falling targets. You can get much the same effect by placing the toe of the butt plate in the center of your shoulder pocket. This can increase recoil effect, though. I'd recommend that you learn to get your shots off faster.

One more important point: the target that you take from the back line is escaping rapidly by the time your shot catches up with it. Be sure, doubly sure if possible, that you oversweep this bird. On the straightaways, you still shoot what appears to be right at the target, whereas in actuality the comb adjustment you made by adjusting the butt position against your shoulder will place you low enough so that your pattern and the target will meet on schedule for you. But on all deflection shots from the back line, exaggerate your sweep to be certain you get out in front of the bird. Do this one simple thing and you will find that back-line shooting, for all of its bugaboos, can be lived with if you have the nerve.

If skeet shooters have a code of conduct in their own circles, trap men are just as demanding that a set of ground rules be followed. The rules are common sense, as you will see:

1. When you take your shooting station at the trap line, stand there quietly with your gun *open* and unloaded, muzzle down.
2. As the gunner next to you calls for his bird, load your shotgun, but

do not close the action until you shoulder your gun in turn. Merely be ready with a shell in the open chamber when your turn comes so that you do not slow down the shooting rhythm of the rest of the squad.

3. As in skeet shooting, call for your bird clearly, saying "Pull." No grunts or growls are required as a substitute.

4. After you have fired at your target, eject your empty round promptly and return your gun to rest position until it becomes your turn once again.

5. Trapshooting requires that you change shooting stations after you have fired 5 rounds. The referee will tell you when to move, and when he does, be alert and do so promptly.

6. In the event of a jam or malfunction, keep the gun pointed out over the outfield while you either clear it or call for assistance. Do not leave station until it is cleared of all live rounds.

7. When someone is shooting somewhat less than well on your squad, keep your advice to yourself. It may very well be that the gentleman may ask you what in blazes he is doing wrong. If he does, talk it over after the round is completed so that you do not disturb the other members of the squad.

Trap is a fun game if you approach it with that in mind. As with skeet, if you let trapshooting become an obsession, your field gunning will suffer. Trap is an excellent polisher of deflection shooting, however, and used on this basis, can be a means of practice for you that is hard to beat.

PLATE 61. Keep your advice to yourself. No shooter could possibly care less why you think he missed that last target.

9 | FIELD SAFETY AND MANNERS

There is no excuse whatsoever for a hunting accident. A hunting accident is nothing more than a breach of standards, either of courtesy or of attention. The field is no place for a man who is guilty of either sort of violation.

How our grandfathers, men who hunted daily with hammer shotguns, old muzzle-loaders at that, ever grew to the ripe old age of reproduction is a matter of total amazement to me. In all my years of shooting, the closest I ever came to meeting my maker was with an exposed hammer weapon in the hands of a person who didn't much give a damn for anyone but himself. The instant you carry a hammer into the open where brush and careless hands can get at it, you are begging for trouble.

Modern shotguns designed and built by reputable manufacturers are almost invariably mechanically safe. I say "almost invariably" because there's always a minute possibility that any manufactured item, no matter who designed and built it, may have a flaw. However, in accidents involving guns, it's almost always the person handling the gun who is at fault, rather than the firearm.

Normally the only way a shotgun can be fired is to move the safety to the off position and pull the trigger. One September many years ago, I pointed out an exception to this rule to Pete Kuhlhoff, then *Argosy* magazine's top-notch gun editor. We were in Arizona for the opening days of their spectacular dove shooting. Along about midmorning the shooting had slowed and we were picking birds at our stand. I happened to mention that the pump gun he was using would fire if the safety was off and the trigger depressed when the bolt was slapped shut. Pete looked quizzical. Picking up his shotgun, I opened the action and slipped a shell into the chamber. Then, pointing the barrel skyward, I depressed the trigger and slammed the bolt forward into lock. The resultant blast brought Pete directly to his feet—a monumental project for a man 6 feet 8 inches tall who weighed close to 300 pounds.

"Wow!" Pete said. "I never saw that done before." Which proves that even after close association with shotguns you can still be ignorant of something important. Since then, that model shotgun has been redesigned to make it impossible to fire in that manner.

Skeet automatics, or for that matter any automatic (semiauto, to be precise) will *usually* not fire when the action is closed, safety off. I say "usually" because one bit of grit, residue of old powder, or dirt on the firing-pin traveler can hold it out enough to discharge a shell when the firing pin strikes the primer. A double, one that breaks at the breech, is perhaps the safest of all shotguns to carry. To begin with, your rounds are immediately visible when you open the breech. Second, the base of the barrels rides down in such close proximity to the breech face where the firing-pin holes are that any projecting parts of these pins are struck by the barrel base and either depressed, or the gun will not shut.

In the chapter on gun pointing, I mentioned that you should seldom look directly at a given object in the field; rather you should take in the field as a whole. This is doubly important when you hunt with other people or dogs. The instant your attention becomes riveted to a bird or a bunny on the gallop, you shut out anything else that might lie *beyond* your target. Let this habit take hold of you and you become a tragedy looking for a place to happen. Consider the following episode as a case in point, if you will.

The early years of my shotgun handling were hectic affairs of many rounds for minimal results. I was fast, ever so fast, but I had great difficulty finding that place where target and charge were to meet. One thing I was if nothing else—ever conscious of my hunting companions. The day I killed my first grouse points this up more thoroughly now than it did then.

Dad and I were hunting a creek bottom together, working toward a peninsula that we had set up as our flushing point for the birds we had moved down the bottom. Dad was next to the creek while I skirted the hemlocks about fifty feet away. A grouse roared out of the cover ahead and swung sharply back between us. My little 16 over-and-under jumped into position at my shoulder as I tracked the bird and then, there it was—Dad's bright red hunting hat right smack over the barrel. I lifted the gun to clear him, lowered it once again, and killed the bird before it reached the heavy cover behind us. Dad walked over and shook my hand warmly. He never once mentioned the fact that he had died a little when he saw that barrel cross him, but he did mention the fact that he saw the barrel rise, clear him, and then resettle into shooting position. This is nothing more than good shooting habits built in at an early age.

Just as in driving a car, where you watch the car in front of you *and* the car directly in front of him, knowing the exact location of your hunting com-

panions and the bird dogs you are following is far more important than the game you bag in a day afield. I have passed up shots I could have made easily for the simple reason that I was not sure precisely where my partner was in heavy cover. No bird is worth taking a chance on injuring anyone.

A shotgun wound is a hideous affair, full of tearings and complete destruction of tissue at close-range contact. It is extremely difficult for even the most accomplished surgeon to repair—I have talked to many who have had the unpleasant experience of trying. Such a wound usually occurs at a ghastly range—under 10 yards. The attendant bleeding is enormous with excessive loss of blood as standard. Struck in the upper body area with a shot charge, a man has scant chance of survival to reach a hospital, let alone the operating room. *You can inflict this on your partner!*

Most of us have seen, at one time or another, the Ten Commandments of Safety issued by the National Rifle Association. The country is flooded with these simple rules, yet we continue to have hunting accidents. Do you know the particular set of conditions under which most shotgun accidents occur? They will astonish you as they did me. The visibility is perfect, not more than one tenth obscured. The cover is light, not heavy. The range is *inside* 20 yards on hunter-to-hunter woundings or killings.

Safety rules are so simple, so logical, so all-important that we tend to accept them and pass them over as our confidence in our guns increases with usage. Familiarity should never breed contempt for common sense, but it does. And when you analyze these rules of safe gun handling, you may see, in the mirror of your memory, yourself reflected as a violator. If such is the case, shape up, my friend! Here they are, with some thoughts on each:

1. *Treat every gun with the respect due a loaded gun.* This is logical to the extreme. A gun is not the cause of hunting accidents; the idiot behind it is. A shot shell has no conscience; it merely carries out the mission built into it. It is designed to kill.

2. *Carry only empty guns, taken down or with the action open, into your automobile, your camp, or your home!* In the kitchen wall of a close friend of mine there is still an obvious scar, one he has left there as a daily reminder. This wall received the full charge of a shotgun when his teen-age son snapped the hammer before opening and checking to see if the gun was empty.

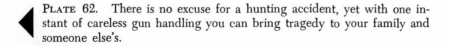

PLATE 62.   There is no excuse for a hunting accident, yet with one instant of careless gun handling you can bring tragedy to your family and someone else's.

My hunting partner can hand me a closed shotgun and I will point the barrel away from him, open the action, check the magazine and/or barrels —all of this while knowing full well he has done it himself. Any shotgun I pick up gets the same meticulous examination, even my own.

For that one reason, I did not kill a close friend this past dove season.

I use a Model 12 Winchester 20-gauge as my meat gun. It is skeet bored, and a lovely little thing to shoot. It was also the recipient of some hard use that year; the action was full of grit and weed seeds, and the magazine the same. We had finished a field, and, casing the guns after emptying them, had gone to another location. Walking around to the back of the station wagon, I slipped my skeet gun out of the carry case, thumbed a round into the chamber, and shut the action. Turning the gun over, I began to insert a shell into the magazine opening. There, right smack in front of my terrified gaze, was the lip of a live round protruding from the magazine tube, a round that had been hung up *inside* the magazine all through the short trip. But for the fact that I follow stringent handling rules with a gun, I could have fired that round accidentally.

3. *Always be sure that the barrel and action are clear of obstructions.* Snow! Brother, if there is one cause of barrel failure in a shotgun, it is the lodging of three to five inches of packed snow in the muzzle. When I am hunting in winter conditions, I constantly check my barrel to see to it that all is clear for that charge to find its way out the other end. The same applies to a fall in the field. If you do fall, stop right there. Clear your gun of all live rounds and then check the barrel. Even a stick wedged down the muzzle can do the job. Take that one minute and be sure.

4. *Always carry your gun so that you can control the direction of the muzzle, even if you stumble.* While this was mentioned in the chapter on gun carries, it bears repeating. Rough terrain makes for uneven, chancy footing. Your gun should positively be under constant control, even if you are on your way to falling flat on your face.

5. *Be sure of your target—and what is beyond it—before you pull the trigger.* To be sure of one's target before firing is good advice, but it isn't comprehensive enough. It's vital to be sure also of what lies beyond or directly beneath your target. Sure, I can kill a bird with you in line—kill him dead. But part of my charge, the edge of the pattern that did not strike my target—that's what buries itself in your protesting anatomy. And that hurts even if it isn't fatal!

◀ PLATE 63. Always check the action and the barrels for live rounds before putting your gun away at the end of the day.

6. *Never point your gun at anything that you do not intend to shoot.* Gawd save us all from TV gun-handling practices. The hero yanks his trusty smoke pole and plays games with it, twirling it around his finger by the trigger guard and the like. He gets shot neatly (and painlessly) in the shoulder to rise and defeat six men in hand-to-hand combat. It makes me ill.

A shotgun wound is one helluva hole, regardless of where you place it. It also hurts as if the very devil had bitten you. You do not rise after being struck with the multiple-shock effect of a charge; rather, it knocks you kicking. It is not the *Bang! You're dead* game that we all played as kids. It is very damned permanent.

Nothing angers me more than to have some brat shove a toy gun in my middle and say "Stick 'em up!" Sure, it's only a game. Sure, he doesn't know that real guns kill . . . but why not? Is it because his father didn't raise the roof when he found him in his bedroom one day playing stick 'em up with

PLATE 64.   Be sure not only of your target but also of what lies beyond or directly beneath your target before you pull the trigger.

Daddy's favorite goose magnum? I don't like the attitude that children have in this electronic age of ours that death is clean and normal. Once you see a man die, you change your views on this subject rapidly.

Teach yourself and yours to follow this rule above all others. When you point that barrel at something, you intend to kill it. If you do not, don't point. It is that simple.

7. *Never leave your gun unattended unless you unload it first.* Great rule . . . one of the best. If you are not using a weapon, take the live rounds out of it before you lay it down. Basic? You bet!

8. *Never climb a fence with a loaded gun.* I guess we've all done this at one time or another. A lot of hunters still do it. And each year, some of them die. At best, this is a stupid reason for shuffling off this mortal coil; at worst, the results can be horrible to contemplate. Consider how your family will feel when some strange officer knocks at the door and tells them that an ounce and a quarter of high velocity 6's has taken off most of your face. Sure, you'll be beyond caring then, but what about them? It takes only a few seconds to remove the shells from any hunting gun, but that simple act could mean many more seasons afield for you.

9. *Never shoot at a flat, hard surface or at the surface of the water.* That hair-raising *ping* you hear on television after a bullet strikes a rock is rarely if ever heard after a charge of shot is fired. But that doesn't mean shot doesn't ricochet from hard surfaces. Its remaining velocity is usually low enough so it's silent, but it can still be dangerous to others or even yourself.

Over a dozen years ago, Dad and I were hunting on one of those miserable frozen days that you encounter occasionally in Eastern winter weather. We were prowling about a frozen swamp bottom when I jumped a cottontail. The bunny took off straight away from me and at least 20 feet out of direct line of fire to Dad. Checking him, I rolled the rabbit only to hear him yell, "Ouch, goddammit!" He stood there rubbing his bottom while I walked over to see what had happened. The charge had struck one of those frozen hummocks on an angle and then ricocheted back over that safe 20 feet of slack. But *it was nearly spent* when it struck him.

This is a good rule.

10. *Never mix gunpowder and alcohol.* You'd better believe it. No one on the face of this earth likes a posthunt belt any better than I do, but that comes *after* the guns are unloaded and cased and we are home again. Never before. Anyone who drinks and hunts is a damned fool that I want no part of, any time, any place.

An outdoor writer sees more gun safety violations than most hunters. He hunts with a number of different people all over the country. When

PLATE 65.   Never climb a fence with a loaded gun. Here the man about to climb through the fence is handing his gun to his partner. Such team-work can eliminate any possibility of a close-range shooting accident.

one happens (or starts to happen), I will climb all over a man (or woman) breaking a safety rule either inadvertently or on purpose. Being polite does nothing more than hasten the day when the accident happens—and happen it must.

Some years ago I was hunting in a northern prairie state, then one of the country's top pheasant regions. I should have come away with memories of the great hunting, but what stands out clearest in my mind is a frightening practice common there. Come late afternoon, the custom was to pick up the last few birds of the day by easy road hunting. Several men pile into an automobile and ride the section line roads, looking for pheasants in the ditches and shelter belts. The gun type favored there is a pump or autoloader bored modified or full. The locals clear the chamber but leave the magazine full. This amounts to nothing more than traveling with a loaded gun in the car, an unsportsmanlike habit at best, and one that can be highly dangerous. When a bird is seen, the driver pulls over and one or more men pile out, working a round into the chamber as they hurry to get a shot. It takes little imagination to realize that sooner or later an overanxious gunner is going to chamber a shell before he's actually out of the car, and in the crowded confines he'll hit the trigger. The best that can be hoped for then is a ragged hole in the car roof. The worst I would rather not contemplate.

I don't mean to single out these Midwestern hunters for special criticism. Many of us have bad habits and this one illustrates the point that nobody's gun handling is perfect. I don't want to preach, but it's obvious we must all make a special effort to eliminate any actions which can have unexpected and deadly results.

As a good shot, you earn the respect and admiration of a number of other hunters not so fortunate. Such a mantle demands that it be worn with grace and pride. It does not lend itself gracefully to poor gun-handling practices. Therefore, if we must put forth a syllogism, a good shot must be a good gun handler. One follows where the other steps.

Be prideful of ability, for pride makes you strive to improve on that ability. But never let pride become arrogance, for in arrogance lies trouble. Once you feel that you are above rules, that you are so perfect that rules no longer apply to you, but just to the common herd, *look out!* We all can tongue-in-cheek-it and say that rules are made to be bent. Possibly they are—everywhere except with a loaded gun in your hands. Then, all rules must be followed. There is no tomorrow after a mistake!

EPILOGUE

My desk looks like a disaster area and my eyes feel as if I had been at this for years rather than months. But what I wanted to say is all here. There are some who may disagree with me, but I have to stick to what I feel is right. I know what I set down here is right for me and that it will work for you . . . given the chance.

I wish I could stand at your elbow and help you over the rough spots—for you will encounter them, as have all of us. Not being able to do so, all I can say is that if you want to become a better than average shot, you can. Your degree of accomplishment will depend entirely upon your own efforts. If they are conscientious and well directed, you cannot help coming out a winner.

THE LAKE
WILLIAMSPORT, PENNSYLVANIA

INDEX

Illustrations are indicated by italic numbers

from GEZA

Richard K. Geyer

1983